SANTA BARBARA LIVING

SANTA BARBARA LIVING

Diane Dorrans Saeks
and the Editors of **Santa Barbara Magazine**

Principal Photography by Lisa Romerein
Foreword by Jennifer Smith Hale

RIZZOLI
NEW YORK

Halcyon days
--Diane Dorrans Saeks

Cover: Diandra Douglas's classical garden and pool in Montecito.
Previous pages: Beneath fragrant eucalyptus trees, a languid pool
near Santa Barbara, with furniture designed by Michael Smith.

First published in the United States of America in 2008
by Rizzoli International Publications, Inc.
300 Park Avenue South
New York, NY 10010
www.rizzoliusa.com

2008 2009 2010 2011 / 10 9 8 7 6 5 4 3 2 1

ISBN-13: 978-0-8478-3155-5
Library of Congress Catalog Control Number: 2008925159

Designed by Subtitle

Printed in China

SANTA BARBARA LIVING

CONTENTS

SANTA BARBARA
A LOVE FOR LIFE

By Jennifer Smith Hale

Santa Barbara is a place one falls in love with at first sight. I know this to be true, because it happened to me. I recall the first time I set foot in Santa Barbara. The smell of the night-blooming jasmine, the way the sun hit the Santa Ynez Mountains, creating the most beautiful backdrop, the shimmering expanse of the Pacific— it all had me intoxicated!

Twenty-five years earlier my dad, Robert Nathaniel Smith, then in his late twenties and in an era where political idealism was high, had his own fateful first encounter with Santa Barbara. It was the early 1970s. He'd come out to California from Washington DC to help register as many young voters as possible. His friend Joe Kennedy (whose own uncle John honeymooned in Santa Barbara decades before) took my father to one of the vistas overlooking the city and introduced this magical place to a nice Midwestern boy. It was a view that stayed with him forever, haunting him, a place that was too beautiful to be believed. He dreamed of a way to make it back there one day, of a way to live in such an extraordinary place.

Having always kept California in mind, my father's dream of moving our family came true in 1988. A broadcasting executive, he had an amazing opportunity to run the only television station in town, and he came out to California to close the deal. A day later came the phone call that would change our lives. He had asked a realtor to drive him around Santa Barbara to learn more about different neighborhoods. On the third house of the tour, he found the perfect home: a 1920s Mediterranean, the classic Santa Barbara style house. He bought it on the spot, without even checking with my mother, Anne. He had fallen hard—for the town, the house, and the life this superb locale had to offer.

My family's life in Santa Barbara was as magical as we had dreamed. Everyone we met was so warm and open, and the friends we made quickly became like a second family.

Our house was the center of many wonderful moments, memories, and celebrations. Our family grew closer. My brother and I went away to college, yet we would still be drawn back to that place, to that house, to the love that was waiting there.

After graduation, and newly married to my husband, Nicholas Hale, I returned to this city that I love, at first to work for our family television group. One day, while enjoying lunch together in one of our favorite courtyard restaurants, the Wine Cask, my father and I decided that the best way for us to honor the city that gave us so much happiness would be to purchase and relaunch *Santa Barbara* magazine with a new design and editorial concept. It would be our love letter to this place, a way to share with everyone the treasures that were around every corner, from the perfect antiques store in Summerland to the most wonderful gelato shop, an orchid oasis, or the newest clothing boutique in Montecito. In photographs and stories, we would take readers inside the houses and gardens of this place we called home.

I am thankful for many things, as I have been blessed in this life, but one of the things I am most grateful for is that my father fulfilled his dream of living here. As it turned out, my father, then battling cancer, lived the rest of his life in Santa Barbara—fifteen years of happiness in his hallowed home.

This city, full of so many beautiful things—estates, gardens, courtyards, fountains, mountains, ocean vistas, orange blossoms, red tiles, statues, roses, bougainvillea, stone walls, hedges—as well as accomplished and generous people, is the gift my father left for me. It is my father that I see in all of the city's precious jewels. It is his love and excitement for every beautiful detail that to this day continue to amaze and inspire me.

Santa Barbara, April 2008

DISTANT CHANNEL ISLANDS (Opposite) The redesigned pool on the hillside below Diandra Douglas's historic villa.

INTRODUCTION
THE LATITUDE OF HAPPINESS

By Diane Dorrans Saeks

In Santa Barbara, Montecito, Summerland, and the sunstruck region from Carpinteria to Butterfly Beach and north to Goleta, the majestic landscape inspires admiration. The air whirs with the winged energy of delight.

In the blue hour of twilight in Montecito, the lit taper of birdsong drifts through native black oaks and pine trees. Across the foothills of the Santa Ynez Mountains, the sweet perfumed evidence of spring floats in vapor trails through the light-charged atmosphere. Closer to the coast, estates bask in the late sun on tree-shaded hilltops, inclined toward expanses of silver-struck ocean and indigo-dipped islands.

I set off on a journey to discover secret, insider Santa Barbara, following the nebula of the almost seen. I explored remarkable villas and encountered great houses, and met the accomplished people who created them and those who live among the hallowed walls.

Framed by a dramatic coincidence of light-refracting Pacific Ocean and the chaparral-covered Santa Ynez Mountains, the Santa Barbara landscape is jeweled with houses surrounded by lavish gardens, reserves of ancient trees, horse trails, and clear skies.

A synchronicity of benevolent weather, with morning fog that clears the air, mild winters, and a perfect alignment of stars, offers the best atmosphere for ideas, inspiration, social and cultural generosity, and the high-energy force field that drives residents to build, design, paint, collect, plant, garden, and think in grand and creative ways.

Everywhere the region hurls thunderbolts of beauty, dazzling residents and visitors alike. If there is the smallest quibble with any aspect of living in the region, it is never voiced.

This is not the land of cynics or complainers. It is indeed difficult to find fault with a day that starts at 7 a.m. for a good hour of surfing with friends out in the bay. A Santa Barbara morning can then lead to a productive few hours of work, and effortlessly drift to an evening stroll along the beach, perhaps a horse ride up in the hills, an hour of yoga by the pool, a stop for a taco or two at a street-side stand, or dinner with friends or family on a terrace with ocean views. And this is a day in mid-January, or even March, when across the country storms are lashing the lakeshore in Chicago, blizzards are buffeting Boston, and snow has turned Central Park into a black-and-white Stieglitz scene. Even Los Angeles, just ninety miles to the south, may be shrouded in fog, while Summerland gleams in eternal sunshine.

In Santa Barbara winters, roses are flourishing, jasmine scents the air, young horse-mad girls are grooming their ponies at a sunny stable in Montecito, and, at Il Brolino, a team of gardeners is clipping box hedges in preparation for a weekend charity fund-raising party. Summer means late-evening dining on the terrace, Sunday afternoon drives with the top down, walking the horses in the cool of early morning, and shimmering light lingering until almost midnight.

In this perceptual field, it goes with the territory to appreciate every light-flecked day, and to honor each moment with silent thanks.

SPLENDOR IN THE SUN

Top photographer Michael Haber and his wife, the designer Eileen Haber, moved to the Santa Barbara area in 2004. With their three young children they live in a Spanish Colonial–style hacienda not far from the San Ysidro Ranch.

"In our house we are protected by the Santa Ynez Mountains to the east," said Eileen. "We can see the Pacific Ocean two miles to the west. We are surrounded by grand old California native oak trees. Here we are nurtured by beauty and peace. It's a wonderful place for children to grow, learn, and experience life. The air feels healthy, and we are away from the stresses of the city."

For the great American architect and interior designer John Saladino, living in Santa Barbara was a lifelong dream. As Saladino loves to recall and recount, he first landed in Santa Barbara at the age of sixteen, on a family holiday, and had a *coup de foudre* that never faded in over fifty years.

"We stayed at the grand Biltmore Hotel, and for me, from the Midwest, it was like an apparition, with the ocean steps from the hotel, the mountains framing the stage set, and the intoxicating smell of salt air and eucalyptus," said the designer. "I already knew I was going to be an architect and designer. And I knew I would eventually live in Santa Barbara."

Saladino, originally from Kansas City, went on to graduate from Notre Dame and the Yale School of Art and Architecture. After a detour working in Rome, he founded his own design practice in New York in 1972. Within a decade he was working with clients in Santa Barbara, and house-hunting in Montecito. He has since owned three houses in the area. Today, he lives his ultimate dream in Montecito, in a historically significant stone house dating from the 1920s, among old oaks, gnarled cypresses, and ribbon-bark eucalyptus trees.

"Santa Barbara is as close as you can come to an earthly paradise," said the well-traveled Saladino, who also has residences in Connecticut and on Manhattan's Upper East Side. "Here the weather is relaxing and benign, and serene. We are not crowded, or buffeted by noise."

His neighbors, the Habers, like Saladino, also have a profound appreciation of the history and culture of the Santa Barbara area.

"This is such a soulful place, with a rich and at times dramatic history," said Eileen Haber. "Santa Barbara has depth. We have friends whose families go back many generations in the region. We are surrounded by history, spirituality, inspiration."

BRIGHTNESS VISIBLE

Los Angeles interior designer Michael S. Smith has worked on six major estates in Montecito, and he has a weekend house in the hills near the San Ysidro Ranch.

"For the legendary families from the Midwest and the East Coast who first started building estates in Montecito and Santa Barbara at the turn of the century, the weather and the great expanses of sunny hillsides were a magical experience," said Smith.

These titans of industry would arrive by train to escape a cold winter in Philadelphia or Chicago with plans to build a perfect world in a gentle south-facing climate. A visionary who arrived with a fortune could create his or her dream of the world.

"Here, you put a seed into the ground and a tree grows, a great landscape is born," said Smith.

Families who made their mark included the Armours, the Pillsburys, the McCormicks, the Ludingtons, the Mortons, the Blisses, and the Fleischmans, who all crafted their fortunes with highly profitable quotidian products, as well as the mundane, the glamorous, and the necessary, and went on to live like royalty in noble estates high above Santa Barbara.

The design of these estates required bold surroundings, and the projects soon attracted some of the most talented landscape designers of the early twentieth century. Among them was Lockwood de Forest III, who designed gardens that seventy years later remain precisely as he envisioned them.

De Forest set out for his educational Grand Tour of Europe after graduating from Williams College. His forays and research took him to the great Italian Renaissance palazzi, castles, villas, and formally delineated gardens. Equally important to the history of garden design in Santa Barbara, de Forest (known to friends as Lockie) traveled to Spain and studied the elaborate and graceful plantings, patterns, watercourses, fountains, and tiles of the great Moorish gardens in Granada and Córdoba.

Lockwood de Forest (whose illustrious family included plein-air painters, writers, and interior designers) brought his knowledge back to Montecito, where he planned the fountains and gardens of the Constantia estate, which are still as breathtakingly elegant as they were in the 1920s. De Forest and, later, his wife, Elizabeth Kellam de Forest, designed and perfected many more public and private gardens until he died in 1959 and she passed away in 1984. His influence on later landscape designers such as Florence Yoch and Lucille Council is also apparent. (Il Brolino is their masterwork.)

THE ARCHITECTURE OF JOY

Architect George Washington Smith designed estates that are the gold standard in Santa Barbara. Smith attended the Harvard School of Architecture and after marrying in 1912 set sail to Paris, where he studied art and architecture at the Julian Academy of l'École des Beaux-Arts.

Smith immersed himself in the cultural life of Paris, and researched classical architecture, painting, and landscapes. In 1916 the Smiths moved to Santa Barbara, and soon after, Smith built his own Montecito residence, in the Spanish Revival architectural style, inspired by fabled manor houses of rural Andalusia.

George Washington Smith worked in Santa Barbara for only fourteen years, but his elegant, classical Spanish Revival architecture has been highly influential. Working closely with his draftsperson, Lutah Maria Riggs, who later became a licensed architect, Smith produced plans for more than eighty designs for new or remodeled houses. Sixty were built.

Smith's approach was grounded in his classical training, and was very personal, graceful, elegant, and, in its effect, distinctly Californian. Most residences were based—with a light touch—on Moorish and Spanish precedents, but he also designed in the more classical Greek-inspired Palladian and Italian Renaissance styles.

Smith's finest houses are admired both within the region and nationally. Each residence has a clear and vivid point of view, pronounced integrity, and graceful authenticity. Each today projects elegant silhouettes and confident forms into the surrounding landscape. His influence lingers.

It was George Washington Smith's work that inspired the arched colonnade of artist Gerald Incandela's superb new horse stable in Summerland. The very substantial proportions of the columns were crafted from cast concrete shaped and finished with stucco. Incandela wanted his Andalusian country manor–style building to be a tribute both to Smith and to the Spanish architecture that has become the Santa Barbara vernacular.

"For us it is more than a stable," noted his partner, George Schoelkopf. "For us it's sculpture, an architectural statement with beautiful horses inside it. Well, for Gerald, the horses are the important elements."

Montecito interior designer Christina Rottman is also an admirer of George Washington Smith, and she especially appreciates his talent for evoking a feeling of transcendence.

"I visit Smith's houses and have a feeling of being somewhere else in place and time, not in twenty-first-century California, but perhaps in the Mediterranean or classical Europe," said Rottman, whose firm, Christina Rottman Designs, works with clients all over the region.

"Nothing expresses Santa Barbara style better than Smith's understated elegance," said Rottman. "And the best interior design for these houses is never contrived but rather evolved and collected so that the overall expression is one of layered luxuries and comfort. There is at the same time the magic of an innate architecture and a very tangible sense of our modern, sophisticated life here."

In Santa Barbara, designers are always aware of the

unique relationship of the interior to the exterior. The Spanish-style architecture that is favored opens naturally to embrace the garden, the courtyards, the view, the outdoors.

New interiors honor history and authenticity, not with museumlike rigidity, but with a more vibrant modern expression. Living spaces can be at one moment elegant and grand, and the next casual and tranquil.

Rottman, like other designers, also relishes encountering the exquisite simplicity of design and proportions in the most elegant estates.

"The concept of less is more is fully embraced in Santa Barbara architecture," she said. "There is nothing better than this refined simplicity, with pale plaster walls punctuated by darker details in wood, wrought iron, stone, and tiles. The play of shape and curves in the graceful arches set off by the stricter geometry of the structural columns, roof lines, and balustrades offers a geometry of light and shadow of landscape and creates patterns on a wall outside or through a window."

THE WINGS OF HISTORY

Compared with other regions of the United States, Santa Barbara's architectural history is brief. Spanish architecture, especially in highly art-directed and style-protected downtown Santa Barbara, reminds history-minded residents that in the late 1700s Captain Gaspar de Portola wrote of his march into the area with his band of soldiers at Arroyo Burro, where he was greeted by friendly Indians from several tribes. Archaeologists have found artifacts of Indian life along the coast dating back six thousand to ten thousand years.

In 1769 Spanish soldiers built their Presidio, and Padre Junipero Serra found a spot for California's tenth mission, in Montecito's East Valley. At the time, wolf packs and California grizzly bears were said to roam the hills. From 1782 to 1846 the king of Spain gave soldiers attaining retirement fifty-acre parcels of land (often in lieu of pensions) on which to build, and many of these first families' descendants still live on the properties, or at least on a part of the original land.

Lt. Narciso Fabregat of the Santa Barbara Presidio received a land grant in 1843. The Spanish army's work, at that time, included capturing pirates. Starting around 1850, the earliest settlers from the East galloped triumphantly into town by covered wagon and started building houses. The price of hillside land in Montecito had already risen to fifty dollars an acre by 1867. When the Southern Pacific railroad arrived in 1887, passengers included the first vacationers, as well as health fanatics drawn by hot springs and sunshine.

The fashionable health resort of Santa Barbara soon attracted barons of industry, who brought with them their chosen architects, landscape designers, and craftspeople to construct their castles in the air.

Refined and worldly architecture, formal interiors, elegant landscaped gardens, and professional interior design became the legacy of Santa Barbara in the last decades of the nineteenth century and at the turn of the century, when illustrious families with fortunes made in banking, railroads, petroleum, mining, spices, wool, real-estate speculation, and shipping headed west from New York, Pennsylvania, Boston, and Chicago in search of sun and beaches and endless summer.

From around 1900, spectacular hotels opened, attracting families with notable names such as Peabody, Rockefeller, Cudahy, Carnegie, Morton, Du Pont, and Swift. Many were the founders of American companies with household names that invented products that even today are on grocery and pharmacy shelves, and whose names are reflected daily on stock exchange charts.

Industry leaders escaping the jaws of winter for a few weeks were soon seduced by the sweetly scented scenery. They began buying swaths of hilltops, making two-hundred-acre land grabs, and building the first lavish estates in Montecito.

There was McCormick's Riven Rock, Ludington's Val Verde, Bothin's Piranhurst, Bliss's Casa Dorinda, Peabody's Solano, Gray's Grayholm, and the noble estate Las Tejas.

Santa Barbara reverberated with the hue and arc of summer and winter cultural seasons, grand balls, *vernissages*, galas, concerts by the great Polish pianist Ignacy Jan Paderewski, performances by dance legend Martha Graham, and the creation of country clubs, golf courses, equestrian stables, private clubs, and polo fields.

Hollywood directors and early stars also discovered Santa Barbara, arriving around 1910 to make the first films. Santa Barbara and the hills and undeveloped land surrounding the town were ideal locations, and the region offered stables, mansions, landing fields, and beaches for endless silent movies.

In *Material Dreams*, Kevin Starr's vivid 1990 treatise on the growth and development of southern California through the 1920s, the author, a history professor and California state librarian emeritus, noted that the early architecture was rather wide-ranging, but that it soon found its focus in Mediterranean motifs.

Francis W. Wilson, an early Santa Barbara architect, could perform successfully in Romanesque Revival, American Colonial, Queen Anne, Gothic Revival, Renaissance Palladian, and California Craftsman, noted Starr. In 1917 Wilson created the elegant villa for Las Tejas, still one of the great estates of Montecito. Its lavish gardens, now a national horticultural treasure, were inspired by the formality, architecture, and lush sensuality of Italian Renaissance landscapes.

Like many Montecito estates, Las Tejas began with a dream to recapture the glories of the formal Italian gardens that graced the historic palazzi and villas of Rome and Florence.

"Las Tejas boasted the finest gardens in Montecito," said Starr, an astute historian and a witty essayist. "In its combination of pools, fountains, plantings, terraces, lawns and vistas, the princes and cardinals of Counter-Reformation Italy might have found themselves perfectly at ease."

Montecito and Santa Barbara were fortunate indeed with the arrival in 1893 of the noted Italian horticulturist Dr. Francesco Franceschi (born Emmanuele Orazio Fenzi at his grandfather's Palazzo Fenzi in Florence). He was to leave a lavish heritage of trees and exotic plants throughout the region. It was Franceschi who introduced varieties of Japanese persimmons, figs, purple orchid plants, Italian stone pines, and *Agave attenuata*, along with cherimoyas, Cape chestnut trees, mangoes, coral trees, even Italian vegetables such as the zucchini, all of which he imported from places as remote at that time as North Africa.

Franceschi, a former banker, arrived with a passion for the world of horticulture, and soon immersed himself in his new nursery and arboretum, importing, propagating, collecting, and annotating plants, and planning, planting, and nurturing the early gardens of Montecito with species palms and varieties of bamboos. Franceschi, a bearded gnome of a man, also introduced avocado varieties, dozens of palms, cycads, tropical fruits, and the Montezuma cypress. Franceschi's elegant plant palette included native trees and flowering shrubs, and his use of native and Mediterranean plants set the style for future generations of gardeners, nurseries, garden clubs, and landscape architects.

Franceschi's mansion, Montarioso, still stands on the Riviera. Its garden is a public park. His work lives on also with the "Montecito," rose he hybridized. A graceful climber, his rose blooms with large, very fragrant, single white flowers, in a long-lasting spring flourish. It was created at Franceschi's beautiful hillside residence.

In 1904 the German landscape designer Otto Niedermüller arrived in Santa Barbara to supervise and design La Favorita, the Gould estate. He later collaborated with Lockwood de Forest on Ganna Walska's Lotusland, the emblematic Montecito garden. Dutch horticulturist Peter Riedel set up his own nursery on Hot Springs Road in 1905. He worked on Solano, the Peabody estate, and his plant knowledge and elegant formal plans continued into the 1930s. Each landscape designer and passionate plantsman enriched and enlivened the Santa Barbara landscape with an ardor for beautiful plants.

LANDMARK STATUS

Michael Smith, who has researched all of the great Montecito estates, observed that in the 1920s many of the estates were "more grandly European than Europe."

"Elaborate carved stone mantels, antiques, and art were brought over from Italy, and then Italian craftsmen and landscape designers were commissioned to create fantasy Italian gardens and rooms," said Smith. "There was such an appreciation of the Grand Tour, the artifacts, and arts of Europe. That great inspiration and connoisseurship still exists among my Montecito clients, who also want to be surrounded by beautiful objects that speak of centuries past and eternal beauty."

The heyday of the great houses, the galas, and winter escapes, faded in the 1930s as the Depression affected even this golden paradise. After the events of 1941, fearful of an invasion of the California coast, many Easterners deserted their houses and headed back home.

"In the sixties and seventies, hundreds of the great houses were seen as white elephants, and the gracious Italianate and Spanish Revival styles seemed dated in their opulence," noted Michael Smith. "Suddenly they were out of vogue as the crisp delineation of Modernism swept the country," he said. "Some of them were 'modernized,' tragically, and great estates were subdivided, and their elegance and drama disappeared. Fortunately, in the latter part of the last century, and early in the twenty-first century, new owners are reviving and beautifying the houses. The new approach to design—appreciative and refined—is having a great effect."

Many of the great estates are etched in the memory, and newer houses show their influence.

"Thanks to the early visionaries who left a legacy of great architecture, I am often able to include the centuries-old techniques and craftsmanship they introduced here in a new residence," said Rottman.

"These early architectural works set a precedent for newer commissions, and, from a design perspective, we all benefit."

Eventually, as freeways in southern California were expanded, and the ninety-mile stretch from Los Angeles to Santa Barbara could be driven in less than two hours, the idea of living in Montecito and keeping an office in Santa Monica or Pasadena and commuting two or three days a week became more practical.

The designer and efficient commuter Jules Allen arrived in Santa Barbara from Los Angeles by chance, and she and her husband, Richard Goldstein, turned into beach fanatics, eventually renting a house inches from the beach.

"We became the total beach family, heading down to Butterfly Beach every morning," said Allen. "In Los Angeles we lived ten minutes from Santa Monica Beach, and we never went there. It took moving to Santa Barbara for us to realize how much fun beach living can be."

They also got to know friends and families in nearby ultra-private Montecito, which reveals itself slowly and discreetly. Now Allen and Goldstein work in their home offices, and happily drive to their offices in Los Angeles several days a week, outside rush hour.

"Since we've moved to this area, we've discovered historic estates, private properties behind tall iron gates and long driveways, wonderful accomplished friends, the film festival, concerts, and the superb local restaurants," said Allen. The family is blissfully immersed in schools and play dates, beaches and hiking trails.

AT THE TURN OF THE WORLD

It has been more than half a century since interior designer John Saladino dreamed of living in Santa Barbara after having his Proustian moment at the Biltmore. His madeleine was the Santa Barbara air, fragrant with salt and eucalyptus, and the Spanish architecture.

"Here, the weather is relaxing, the people I meet are happy, beautifully mannered, and generous, and we live among the most handsome and elegant estates in the world," said Saladino. "You simply feel your best here. The afternoon breeze cheers you on, and the light flickers through the eucalyptus trees as you drive up the hills to Montecito. You feel here that all is well with the world."

Antiques dealer Michael Haskell, whose Mexican and Indian antiques are popular with top designers, grew up in Santa Barbara in the idyllic 1950s and 1960s, an avid surfer pursuing the classic endless summer waves and collecting Indian blankets and Mexican pottery. Eventually he opened his highly regarded eponymous antiques store. Most mornings, if the surf report offers the enticement of a good swell, Haskell, who is now in his seventies, is out surfing. His life in Santa Barbara, it seems, has hardly changed since he was a blond lad clambering down the cliffs to his favorite beach along the Goleta Coast.

"On any day on the water I see old friends from high school, and often I encounter friends from grammar school out catching a wave," he said. "Santa Barbara is a very stable community. There is a great sense of making a home here, living with style and comfort. People like living here, and it is a wonderful place for families. If you left, where would you go?"

Michael Smith, visually hyperattuned, loves the hallucinatory, painterly effect of the clear, bright light as he drives into town along East Valley Road, and then heads up San Ysidro Lane into the foothills of the Santa Ynez Mountains.

"Even the most mundane pastime, such as going to the farmers' market, enjoying a taco downtown, antiquing around Summerland, or visiting used-book stores or design shops, is a pleasure there," said Smith. "Santa Barbara, Summerland, and Montecito are luxurious in the best possible way. Each place has an inherent, authentic beauty. They always live up to their reputation."

John Saladino is ever more passionate about the Santa Barbara area he encountered half a century ago, when he first arrived from the Midwest on a balmy January day.

"The same bouquet of sea salt and eucalyptus that captured me when I was sixteen years old is still as magical," he said. "I loved it then, and I love it now."

Here, he said, echoing every resident's passion, he feels his best. ∎

CHAPTER ONE
GREAT ESTATES

Romantic architectural silhouettes and styles of noble Renaissance Tuscan villas and historic seventeenth-century country fincas of Andalusia inspired the landmark private residences of Santa Barbara.

THE PLEASURES OF CLASSIC BEAUTY

LA QUINTA, the historic residence of Diandra de Morrell Douglas, is one of the treasures of Montecito

Film producer, cultural philanthropist, and champion equestrienne Diandra de Morrell Douglas enjoyed a romantic, fairytale childhood in Deya, a picturesque coastal town on the island of Majorca, off the coast of Spain.

Growing up in a region that Gertrude Stein and poet Robert Graves described as paradise, in the shadow of the rocky Serra de Tramuntana, and with views of the Mediterranean glimmering in the distance, it is not surprising that Douglas has a decades-long fondness for the Santa Barbara area. With its sunny Mediterranean-like climate, whitewashed houses, seaside palazzi, dramatic ocean views, mountain backdrop, and Spanish architecture, the Santa Barbara region is remarkably similar to northwestern Majorca, a jewel in the Mediterranean.

"I grew up in Majorca with writers and painters and archaeologists," Douglas has commented. And it is probably inevitable that she would find a house in Montecito and treasure the region's creators, equestrians, and intellectuals, along with the arts and culture of the Santa Barbara area. As a young girl, she attended several boarding schools, including one in Santa Barbara. For many years her parents, an American diplomat and his wife, a Spanish artist and writer, owned a house on

A SENSE OF ELEGANCE (Opposite and Above) La Quinta has always provided Diandra Douglas with a sense of peace and privacy, with its enclosed terraces and sunny patios, all facing the ocean. Douglas herself, a world-class equestrienne, takes great pleasure in breeding Lusitano horses, and is shown here riding her Lusitano stallion. She has ridden horses since she was a young girl.

RELAXING THE DÉCOR (Opposite and Above) Over several years, Diandra Douglas has updated and simplified the décor of La Quinta, switching out glamorous silk-upholstered tufted sofas for more relaxed cotton-duck slipcovered sofas and chairs. Nonetheless, a modern luxe is assured with gauffraged and silver-thread–embroidered velvet pillows and throws, a bold antique Chinese table, and a pair of gilded Italian chairs with silk velvet upholstery. Above the antique French limestone fireplace stands a pair of Phoenician urns. On the wall of the living room hangs an eighteenth-century Belgian tapestry with a dramatic depiction of a black Spanish stallion, a recurring theme in Douglas's life.

Mountain Drive in Montecito. Douglas graduated from the University of California–Santa Barbara, with a degree in liberal arts studies.

Years later, when she married actor Michael Douglas, the couple acquired the landmark La Quinta, a hilltop villa in the Mediterranean style, built in 1922.

Grace Hayne, a Social Register northern California resident, commissioned the house from Carlton Monroe Winslow, a Boston architect who had arrived in San Diego in 1912 to manage the architecture and buildings for the Panama-California Exposition. A select handful of Spanish-style houses he designed in San Diego are on the historical landmarks register there.

Winslow was from the Boston architectural firm Cram, Goodhue, and Ferguson (still in operation more than a century after its founding in 1898), which had designed libraries, churches, state buildings, and other significant buildings around the country. Though

Winslow subsequently also designed the nearby eighty-room Bliss mansion, Casa Dorinda, it was unusual for him to have devoted his time to La Quinta, a smaller commission. Grander buildings were the forte of his firm. The beautifully calibrated mood and integrity of the Spanish Colonial Revival quinta suggest that Winslow traveled to Spain to study specific and eccentric aspects of correct proportions, detailing, finishing, and siting for the residence on its eight-acre site. Italianate gardens, typical of the Renaissance landscapes popular in Santa Barbara in the 1920s, were also planned and planted on its hillside setting.

Terra-cotta tile roofs, broad sunny terraces, a large swimming pool, arched portals, sunny patios, timbered ceilings, and palm-shaded porches—all with some of the best views of the Channel Islands and fog banks along the horizon—make this one of the most beautiful properties in Montecito.

Around the dining table, Diandra Douglas, whose primary residence is now in New York and who visits Santa Barbara as often as possible, has much to discuss.

Douglas, who was married to Michael Douglas for twenty-three years, is a generous supporter and benefactor of a broad range of educational and cultural causes. She has received special humanitarian awards from the Red Cross.

She runs her own film production company, Wildwolf. She is a generous supporter of UC–Santa Barbara, and is a member of the Chancellor's Council and an elected trustee of the UCSB Foundation. She has also been an admired and creative board member of the Santa Barbara International Film Festival since 1998.

Douglas, a fashion designer, also breeds and sells rare Lusitano stallions, which she keeps at a ranch in the Santa Ynez Valley. The equestrienne recently had a herd of twenty mares and stallions and their ten offspring. She goes out to visit her precious horses, to relax, and to practice dressage privately and gracefully and with great focus in a small arena, with Spanish guitar music playing counterpoint on a stereo.

Meanwhile, she continues to work on La Quinta.

In 1916, California architect Irving Gill wrote, "We should build our house simple, plain and substantial as a boulder, then leave the ornamentation to Nature, who will tone it with lichens, chisel it with storms, make it gracious and friendly with vines and flower shadows as she does the stone in the meadow."

Gill, who is often mentioned in architecture circles in the same breath as Frank Lloyd Wright and is considered one of the major architectural conceptualists of the early twentieth century, would have loved La Quinta. The house has weathered storms, smiled through earthquakes, and adapted to changing times and styles with ease, and is today friendly and inspiring. Approaching its tenth decade, La Quinta has aged gracefully and superbly. ■

THE PERCEPTUAL FIELD
(Opposite) A muted color scheme
in the living room allows antiques
and notable antiquities to be
shown to advantage. A pair of
eighteenth-century Neapolitan
crystal and gilt wood chandeliers
are from the noted Paris *antiquaire*
Ariane Dandois.

SCALE MODELS (Right)
Georgian silver candlesticks, an
Italian porphyry urn, and antique
Chinese bowls are displayed on a
specimen marble tabletop. The
walls are finished with Venetian
plaster. Bui Simon consulted with
Los Angeles designer Michael S.
Smith on the interiors.

THE SPLENDOR OF SYMMETRY
(Following Pages) The brilliance of
Florence Yoch's landscape design,
with its formal box hedges and
topiaries, is also apparent in its
close harmony with the residence.
Many garden historians consider
her landscape for Il Brolino to be
Yoch's finest work. The villa, mostly
unchanged by successive owners,
was originally designed in 1923 by
architect George Washington
Smith for the Wisconsin lumber
heiress Mary Stewart. While the
architect is noted for his Spanish
Revival and Andalusian-style work,
for Il Brolino (the Italian term for
a private garden enclosed by
hedges) his inspiration was classic
noble Italian country villas.

JOY AND LAUGHTER

AT IL BROLINO, their historic Montecito estate, Herb and Bui Simon enjoy the sumptuous glories of the region and celebrate enduring beauty.

Surrounded by eight acres of superbly maintained gardens, pools, elegant statuary, and fragrant terraces, Il Brolino has been one of Montecito's treasures since it was built in 1923.

The work of architect George Washington Smith and landscape designer Florence Yoch, the property has a timeless air, suggesting Renaissance Italy and princely estates in the hills above Florence, mysteriously hidden behind tall stone walls and wisteria hedges. The house, with its shuttered windows, terra-cotta tile roof, and hardy stucco walls, has a rather formal air, more Tuscany than California, despite distant views of the Pacific Ocean beyond the gardens.

When Bui Simon, the new chatelaine, began a two-year complete refurbishment of the residence, beginning in 2002, her plan was to take her cues from the Italian villa and its long traditions of gracious style. With her husband, Herb, a noted philanthropist and real-estate developer, and the designer Michael S. Smith, she made many trips to Rome, Paris, London, and New York in search of the noble and authentic antiques and decorative objects the house demanded.

COSMOPOLITAN MOOD (Opposite and Above) The Simon family enjoys entertaining, and the dining room is often the scene of family get-togethers and celebrations. Its theatrical setting is enhanced by Chinese wallpaper in muted tones. The antique paper, formerly attached to screens, was adapted and restored by Los Angeles artist Doug Funkhauser. The paper depicts village life in a mountain town, with costumed characters, a panoply of robed nobles, and farm animals encircled by tile-roofed cottages among rocky outcrops.

The final effect honors the lineage and grand scale of the house, but feels at the same time comfortable for a family with four young children.

"My favorite time at Il Brolino is when everyone is at home, all the guest rooms are full, and Herb and I can be our most welcoming," said Simon. "Then, every room has its own life. During the holidays our house is filled with music, the children are taking turns at the piano, we all sing along. The house comes alive."

While the house had been decorated with heavy English moldings and the interior had been modified over the years, Simon's focus was on classical Europe and in particular the princely villas decorated over generations, with a cosmopolitan mix of Italian gilded antiques and chandeliers, Dutch mirrors and commodes, Persian carpets, Chinese export and Delft pottery, Florentine marble mantelpieces, and Japanese porcelains.

"Everyone who works on the property—inside and in the garden—has a great sense of pride, and it is in some ways a labor of love," said Simon, a former Miss Thailand (1988) and Miss Universe (1988), and the founder, of Angels Wings Foundation International, a nonprofit group dedicated to helping underprivileged children in Thailand.

"The head gardener has been with the property for more than twenty-six years, and he is the only person allowed to clip the topiaries," said Bui, who noted with pride that the gardener clips them only by hand.

In planning the interiors with Smith, Simon wanted the house to look as if it had always been decorated in the Italian manner.

"It was a treasure hunt to find pairs of chandeliers, the right dining chairs, the perfect dining table, the rugs and carpets with just the right colors and patterns," she

recalled. "We took more than four years, starting with the heart of the house, which has Venetian plaster walls and newly painted Italian Renaissance motifs on the ceilings.

"I am all about the details," said Simon. "The pieces I collected spoke to me. I was prepared to take the time to get the effect we wanted. Now, the rooms tell of our travels to Italy and France, which was how the original owners in the '20s would have decorated."

During the week the family lives in Malibu, where the children attend school. Weekends are spent at Il Brolino.

"It's a wonderful duality," said Simon. "Eventually we will live full-time in Montecito. I am looking forward to that."

Birthday parties and other special occasions are always spent at Il Brolino. "My husband encouraged me to create my dream house," said Simon. "He takes great pleasure in making other people's dreams come true. He has a huge, generous heart. This was a dream for me. We protect the legacy of this wonderful estate. We are very blessed to live there." ■

CREATING EDEN (Right)
The extensive gardens of Il
Brolino were designed by
California-born Florence Yoch
(1890–1972), who drew freely from
Italian Renaissance landscape
ideals and the history and formality
of Florentine gardens. It was Yoch
who in 1939 famously designed
the Tara landscape through which
Vivien Leigh ran in *Gone with the
Wind*. Here in Montecito, Yoch
poised the artifice of clipped
topiaries and box hedges against
the natural hillsides. Yoch's vision
for Il Brolino included a labyrinth
of clipped hedges that invite young
children to explore and play. While
the nine-acre gardens require
daily year-round care by four full-
time gardeners—including the
head gardener who has been
maintaining the property for
twenty-six years—the verdant
planting has several advantages.
The box and Eugenia remain
green all year, and their strict
geometries avoid the passing
prettiness and ephemeral effects
of seasonal flowers. As design
doyenne Diana Vreeland said,
"Style is consistency."

THE GENIUS OF PLACE
(Opposite and Right)
John Saladino's entry gates
bespeak the gravitas of his
approach to design. After a long
steep drive up the hill, guests
experience a thrill and sense of
anticipation and awe at the
grandeur of eighteenth-century
Spanish gates. The gateposts are
reinforced with steel. On top are
Venetian statues of Moses and
St. Jerome.

AFTER LONG SILENCE
(Following Pages)
It was the stone exterior of the
house Wallace Frost designed for
himself in the 1920s that first
entranced John Saladino. It is a
rather theatrical facade, leading
to a small front door that brings
the house down to human scale.
Santa Barbara stone was quarried
on site. The terra-cotta floors
were also made on site. Saladino
replaced the roof, installing
fourteen thousand eighteenth-
century Italian tiles that give the
villa a sense of age and stature.

VILLA SALADINO

DESIGNER JOHN SALADINO'S superb Montecito villa is the full expression of his lifelong love of architecture.

In 1985, visiting Santa Barbara to work with a client, John Saladino saw the stone villa that would became his obsession until he finally owned it in 2001.

The house, crafted in 1930 from local stone by the Alabama architect Wallace Frost, looked as if it had stood on its steep hillside for hundreds of years.

Frost lived and worked in the residence until 1941, when he returned back east.

For six years, Saladino longed for the house, until finally it was for sale, by now an admitted wreck. Windows were broken, there was no heat, and the interiors were garish, with flamboyant coral and teal hues and linoleum tiles covering the terra-cotta floors.

The designer bought the place, out of pure emotion, he said, knowing its restoration would be an enormous undertaking. In the first week, a Santa Barbara pest control crew killed more than two hundred rats. Saladino, who has a horror of vermin, was not deterred. Termites, damp adobe, and collapsing walls were his next challenges.

Over the following months, his sturdy crew continued to clear the property. Pruning and reshaping the twelve-

REALITY IS THE ENEMY OF
GREAT DESIGN (Left)
Among John Saladino's favorite
credos are his beliefs that design
is an illusion, and that good
design requires exaggeration.
The best design, he feels, has an
element of fantasy and refinement.
His sense of the theatrical comes
to full force within the ninety-
year-old stone walls of the living
room of his Montecito villa.
Handsome antique Tuscan chairs
and antiquities are drawn into
service to reveal Saladino's ideal
of an Italian villa, both relaxed
and somewhat formal, with deep-
down satisfying comfort. A pair of
neoclassical urns was bought off
an antique dealer's truck, to
preserve the original weatherworn
finish. Saladino's early-morning
swoop on the dealer's truck
assured that in his hands they
would stay weathered and rustic.
The dealer, Saladino surmised,
would refinish and restore the
urns—erasing the signs of time
that Saladino so prized.

BEAUTIFUL NATURAL LIGHT
IS ESSENTIAL (Opposite and
Right) John Saladino designed his
dining room so that the bright
Santa Barbara light, reflected off
the ocean, would spill into the
room all day. Saladino said in a
recent lecture, "I see furnishings
first as geometry—as squares,
cubes, drums, triangles, and
rectangles, which also happen to
be the silhouettes of sofas, chairs,
tables, lamps, and paintings." He
also noted one of his favorite
design aspirations: that created
spaces should liberate us from
terra firma, allowing spirits to
soar and imaginations to take flight.

acre site, he revealed tree-framed vistas of the ocean.

In two years, Saladino had reinforced the house with steel beams and posts, cleaned ceiling beams, sandblasted paint off stone walls, replumbed, rewired, and finally covered the newly crafted weather-resistant roof with thousands of recycled Italian terra-cotta tiles.

"My position was to make the house seem even older, and to turn it into the antique object, revered," explained the designer.

The project required more than two hundred sheets of plans and drawings.

In close consultation with his design staff, and especially architect Stephen Barlow and senior designer Naoko Kondo, he opened up the interior. Stingy little rooms became luxurious bedrooms and grand salons, each one with Saladino's distinct allure.

With his classical sense of opening the house to acknowledge the outdoors, Saladino installed new windows designed as steel-framed pivoting doors to open to the garden. The stone rooms had a tendency to feel a little muted, so he also added skylights, inviting sunlight, his "prime mover," into the house throughout the year.

But the house was never intended to be a period piece, or a Tuscan stage set.

His interiors continue his philosophy of mixing "old with new," and the complexity of each room demonstrates his full maturity as an artist and a master of scale.

The historical references in the villa offer a rich design education, an instant Grand Tour. His allusions are always implicit. This lover of classicism brings in two thousand years of design references, from the Villa of Mysteries in Pompeii through Palladio and William Kent.

Treasures include antique Flemish crewelwork textiles hanging in the stairway landing, works by Cy Twombly, a

lifetime's collection of books, tall hand-blown vases designed by Saladino, a detailed map of ancient Rome, a rather formal pair of high-back William and Mary chairs acquired at a London auction, along with antique embroidered textiles from Turkey, France, and Belgium.

"I like a certain classicism and formality in my rooms, with a strong sense of proportion and placement—but these rooms must be human in scale and comfort," he said. "I play with scale to give rooms a sense of largesse and grandeur, and in contrast I'll create small vignettes that draw you closer and offer a moment of reflection,

a private moment of repose. This juxtaposition is everywhere in the villa."

Saladino has had a lifelong passion for design. He grew up with a love of art, and was drawing Dick Tracy houses at four years of age. Now nearing his seventieth year, Saladino revels in the beauty he has created in Montecito.

"The sunlight flickers through the trees and I am mesmerized every day," he said. "The bouquet of sea salt and eucalyptus that captivated me when I was sixteen is still here. In Montecito, I've been able to express my deepest dreams. Here I feel my best." ■

THE PURSUIT OF HAPPINESS

A HANDSOME 1895 HOUSE designed by legendary New York architect Stanford White becomes a warm and friendly retreat for a family of avid travelers.

Interior designer Carolyn Espley-Miller and her husband of almost two decades, comedian Dennis Miller, have lived in many delicious corners of the world, including Manhattan, Beverly Hills, and Paris. But when they arrived in Montecito for a wedding fifteen years ago, Carolyn knew it was love at first sight and that this was where she wanted to put down roots and bring up their two young sons.

"Montecito and Santa Barbara seemed like paradise for children, with the wonderful climate, the outdoors, sports, the beach, the healthy air," said Carolyn.

She immediately started looking at properties to rent.

"I convinced Dennis that we could rent a house in Santa Barbara for six months and we would live in Paris the rest of the year," she said. "I started looking at houses with my Realtor, and was not getting anywhere," she

recalled. "Finally my Realtor mentioned a Glen Oaks property for sale, but she discouraged us from looking at it and said it was too big, it needed too much work, and was quite dated. I was immediately interested."

Carolyn drove up and fell in love with the old native oaks, the colonnaded porches, the sunny location on top of a rise, the well-established gardens, and the boy-friendly lawns.

"The bones of the house were great, with large, gracious rooms and a beautiful symmetry and balance," she noted. "It is such a sunny house, and it is large at 10,000 square feet, but it never feels ostentatious. I immediately put down a deposit. We closed escrow when we were in Paris. Dennis had not even seen the house. He trusted my opinion that it would be a wonderful family house."

The house had been built as a winter escape for the family of New York residents Dr. Alexander Blair Thaw and his artist wife, Florence, in 1895. The Thaws, originally from Pennsylvania, engaged architect Stanford White to design their house.

Dr. Thaw was one of a family of eleven children who were heirs to a vast fortune from Pittsburgh Coal and the Pennsylvania Railroad. Thaw commissioned White to design a twenty-one-room shingled home upon the oak-covered acreage for his family and named it Field House. White was the architect most famous for creating New York City's original Madison Square Garden as well as the Washington Square Arch.

The estate became the glamorous setting for many turn-of-the-century society events for several years, until 1907, when Dr. Thaw sold Field House to James H. Moore, financier and president of the Rock Island Railroad, and his wife, Lora. The Moores renamed the estate Glen Oaks because of its woodsy beauty. Lora later became one of the principal financiers of Charles Lindbergh's *Spirit of St. Louis*. Lindbergh visited her on at least two occasions in Montecito, once landing a small single-engine plane on a grassy field west of Ladera Lane.

"When we acquired it, the house had been owned by only four families, and had not been remodeled since the '70s, when ceilings were lowered in an awkward attempt at modernization," said Carolyn. "The floors were covered in a green shag carpet, and there was Brady Bunch wallpaper everywhere. It still felt somehow inviting, even though the colors and styles that seemed so fresh and modern in the '70s were quite horrendous thirty years later."

For Carolyn Espley-Miller, the house was all promise. An experienced and focused interior designer, she knew that the key would be to appraise the style and original intent of the house, and listen to the voice of the architecture.

"It is very much an East Coast–style house, with none of the usual grace notes of Spanish Revival you

NEW YORK TRANSPLANTS (Opposite and Above) All of the furniture in the library and study, including a pair of venerable leather club chairs, antiquarian books, and a dramatic branch of coral, were transported from the Millers' Upper West Side townhouse. The striped wallpaper is by Ralph Lauren Home. The 1896 poster by Parisian caricaturist PAL celebrates traditional mid-Lenten revelries and a rollicking artists' cavalcade through Montmartre, ending with a legendary masked ball at the Moulin Rouge. Dennis Miller insists that the dancer in the poster is in fact Geena Davis, the actress, who was formerly a resident of the nearby Las Tejas estate.

encounter along every road in Montecito," said Espley-Miller. "I took my design cues from the architect."

Carolyn and Dennis had a three-year-old toddler, and she was pregnant with their second son, but she was undaunted, and embarked on what was to be an eighteen-month renovation. The goal, nonetheless, was to end up with a house that felt authentic, its integrity intact.

"I reoriented the front entrance and remodeled the kitchen, but the main rooms are as they originally were planned—with the lowered ceilings removed, of course," said Espley-Miller.

Her color palette included soft tones of apricot, terra cotta, pale cream, and celadon, white, and pale buttercream.

"They are colors that look beautiful in all seasons, and which adapt well from day to night," she said.

Espley-Miller's British heritage shows in her selections of Anglo-Indian furniture, including cane chairs, a rosewood ottoman, and a butler's tray, as well as Georgian silver.

"I love the house in the late afternoon in summer when the sun is golden and reflecting off the ocean," said Espley-Miller. "It is perfect at Christmastime, with its East Coast feeling, the banisters to decorate with greenery, and the carved stone fireplaces lit," she said. "The rooms feel so gracious for entertaining. I go mad with a traditional tree with antique ornaments, pomander balls, and flickering light bulbs."

The Millers are enthusiastic travelers, and recently returned from Bhutan, Rajasthan, and Paris.

"We travel and immerse ourselves in other cultures and landscapes—and then return to this wonderful house," said Carolyn. "This has been a great family house, with many memories."

In 1995 the Miller family purchased the adjoining one-acre property on which the original estate's "recreation house" is located. In November 1995 the Millers were presented with a beautification award from the Montecito Association in appreciation of their efforts to restore the historic Montecito estate. ■

WINGED ENERGY OF DELIGHT

CHRISTINA ROTTMAN'S COSMOPOLITAN DESIGN brings the glamour and exoticism of Morocco and Spain to a family house in the hills of Montecito.

Santa Barbara interior designer Christina Rottman gives credit where it is due.

Architect Don Nulty created the design and exquisite detailing of the superb 9,500-square-foot Moroccan-Spanish–style house her clients acquired in Montecito. The two-and-a-half-acre property, as planned by the Santa Barbara architect, included the elegant house, a guest house, a swimming pool, and a tennis court.

The new owners are a financial consultant and his wife and four young children, relocating from Connecticut.

"Don Nulty planned the wonderfully romantic and fully realized house in 2002, for the previous owners. Don planned the Moorish-Andalusian farmhouse style here,

with every detail perfected. I was very inspired by this house," said Rottman. Originally from the Bay Area, she had studied design with Linda Chase and Peter Carlson in Los Angeles. She also apprenticed with Anouska Hempel in London, so she is well schooled in a range of disciplines and styles.

Rottman admired the integrity and authenticity of Nulty's work; he is noted and popular for the academic rigor he brings to architecture in the region.

"The house was almost a fantasy of Spain and North Africa, with antique architectural elements; traditional handcrafted ironwork, lanterns, arched doors, and windows, overscale doors, graceful balconies, and beautiful

REFINEMENT AND POLISH
(Opposite) In the finely calibrated living room, Christina Rottman replaced a bombastic faux-stone fireplace with a more refined limestone fireplace in the Andalusian style. The walls were hand-finished with a chalky matte plaster with an integral pale chamois tone. The Spanish-style ottoman, by Formations, Los Angeles, is covered with faun suede. The pair of antique white ceramic Chinese garden stools is from Inner Gardens, Los Angeles. The table, left, is by Rose Tarlow. The Khotan carpet is in tones of tobacco, celadon, and ocher.

(Left) Gauffraged silk velvet handcrafted by Irish-French textile designer Sabina Fay Braxton illuminates and enriches the pillows and a throw in the living room and contrasts with the plain suede, velvet, and linen in the room.

stonework," noted Rottman. "That degree of detail and individuality lends itself to creating something fabulous and magical in the interiors."

Still, it was never her intention to turn this into theme design.

"My design is never thematic," she said. "But it does show my love of fashion. Fashion was my first love, and I worked for Valentino for many years, so my couture background often comes into my design."

Rottman viewed the living room as a space for a couple to chat, or for small groups, family celebrations, or cocktail parties.

"Design must transcend time," she said. "In the new gallery, I can see the couple having a candlelit dinner, or when the children grow older they can push the tables and chairs aside, play music, and dance. The current décor can evolve and suit all of those purposes well."

Rooms are enhanced by the deft use of rich neutral colors.

"I always keep the background quite neutral," said the designer. "Then I add just one or two other colors. The key is to enrich rooms with beautiful, tactile textiles and details that delight the eye—on walls, with antiques, and with subtle mixes of antiques, glass, and silver."

"I create spaces, like the new gallery, which was formerly a pass-through space, a breezeway, so that they have many uses, not just one single prescribed use," said Rottman. "I design for the continuous enjoyment over the life of the house, and families change as children grow."

The new gallery had a series of archways on each side, framing the long space. Rottman dressed them in an artful style, with curtains hanging from very thin iron rods and fine iron rings.

"I designed the curtains in two colors, with cream-colored linen by Rose Tarlow on the top and the lower section in a terra-cotta linen twill with a Rogers & Goffigon paprika-colored velvet trim to add an

A COSMOPOLITAN APPROACH (Opposite and Above) In a formerly undefined breezeway upstairs near the children's bedrooms, Christina Rottman created a striking and versatile gallery where the children play games, the family gathers for cards, and the children can study. She designed the carpet with a Moroccan tile pattern, in homage to the Moroccan influences in the house. Game tables in ebonized ash from Brenda Antin in Los Angeles are surrounded by chairs with slipcovers of Rogers & Goffigon linen. The glass lanterns were invented by Joseph Stoddard from antique French garden cloches. Santa Barbara architect Don Nulty designed the Moroccan arch for the doorway to the kitchen. Cabinets are accented in soft sky blue.

architectural element," she said. The trim—which gives the curtains the effect of a wainscot—lines up with the window mullions.

The curtains were also crafted to articulate and define the architecture of the gallery and frame the chairs, with their striped slipcovers.

"I design a room with unexpected antiques and a mix of old and new, so that it looks like a lifetime collection, and pieces from different points of time and place," said the designer. "The idea is always to gather beautiful objects and custom-made décor with special details, and to layer elements, silhouettes, textures, and tones, old and new. Each beautiful piece relates elegantly, and can inspire my clients to continue to collect more art and objects."

In the meantime, Rottman is thinking in terms of both form and function.

"I bring the bones of the interior and I make sure it works for them," she said. "But it is open-ended."

She clarified the interiors so that each space moves effortlessly into the next.

"My clients love this house, and they always tell me it continues to surprise and delight them," said Rottman. ∎

GOLDEN IDYLL

AT LAS ENCINITAS in Montecito, interior designer Michael S. Smith reimagined a Portuguese-style quinta.

Las Encinitas, a Portuguese-style manor, was built in Montecito on the oak tree–shaded grounds of the late-nineteenth-century Pillsbury family estate. With views of the ocean and the mountains, it is one of the classic properties of Montecito, although not yet a decade old.

The architecture, by Tichenor & Thorp and Ferguson & Shamamian, and the interior design, by Los Angeles designer Michael S. Smith, were inspired by explorations of and research into the architecture of the interior of Portugal, and up-close views of the handsome centuries-old quintas (country manors) in the Portuguese hinterlands.

"The main house is quite formal, but with the outbuildings, including guest quarters and a pool house, I was able to be more eccentric," said Smith.

Set among nearly eight acres of carefully tended mature gardens, the buildings draw characteristic architectural details from historic Portuguese quintas, including stucco exteriors, terra-cotta tile roofs, mullioned windows with stone surrounds, blue and white tile wainscots, French terra-cotta tile floors, and limestone fireplaces.

"The plan was to give the residence and the guest suites a very elegant rustic, handmade feeling, more country than city," said Smith.

In the eighteenth century, the Portuguese, always great explorers and traders, ruled an empire stretching from Brazil to Macau to Africa and beyond.

For the interiors, Smith selected a worldly collection of antiques, including Spanish chests, Italian villa tables, Venetian paintings (acquired in London), French portraits, and Dutch and Chinese pottery and paintings. Understated architectural details and noble oaks billowing outside the windows prevail to make it feel very Old World.

Rooms of the residence and guest suites are oriented toward the verdant setting. French doors open onto

PORTUGUESE INFLUENCES

(Opposite and Right) Interior designer Michael Smith and the owners of this landmark property traveled to Sintra, Cascais, and the Douro Valley in Portugal to view historic Portuguese quintas, with their distinctive Baroque exteriors and rather understated but entrancing interiors often cooled and decorated with tile walls. The climate and vegetation of northern Portugal and southern California are quite similar, and the Iberian architecture, with its cooling terraces and emphasis on the outdoors, translates well to Montecito. Blue tiles on the wall, with traditional patterns, are Portuguese classics. Opulent antiques contrast with the simple lines of the architecture, by Tichenor & Thorp as well as Ferguson & Shamamian. The Venetian painting attributed to Tintoretto shows the Doge's gilded barge, a symbol of Venetian power and nobility. It was acquired at the Hackwood Hall country house sale. The leather-upholstered gilt chair, right, was formerly in the collection of Babe Paley.

sheltered courtyards overlooking lily ponds, rose gardens, and fountains. Covered porches in the pool house, and broad shaded loggias in the residence, overlook the gardens.

The residence, fragrant with climbing roses and jasmine, includes superbly furnished living and dining rooms, and a media and game room. There are also a sitting room, a fully furnished library with a fitted cherrywood bookcase displaying a collection of signed first editions, his-and-hers dressing rooms and baths, and a light-filled bedroom with a balcony overlooking lily ponds and lawns. For the residents there is also a Portuguese-style country kitchen and an informal breakfast room.

The quinta and outbuildings were built partially on the original foundations, but in the end little of the 1890s Mission Revival house was salvageable. It had been so aggressively remodeled in the 1970s that it was of little interest. It was also poorly sited, said Smith, and had little remaining character, though the centuries-old foundation worked as a starting point for the new house.

"Each residence must have its own voice and its special character that are appropriate to the location, the climate, and the reality of life and the times," said Smith. "For this house we were inspired by Portugal, but we were not intending a line-for-line copy. The enemy of personal style is conformity. People plan a full-on theme design, such as line-for-line 'French country,' and this can be a mistake. You have to end up with rooms that are bigger, more expansive in ideas and concept. The best design has no name—it's your design, your house, your ideas."

Smith and the architects drew up a rambling one-level house with views, quiet courtyards, and terraces.

"When you are translating traditional architecture, it is essential to borrow and be inspired in a way that is not tricky or museumlike," he said. "We wanted architecture that felt sophisticated and polished, somewhat

understated and refined, not heavy-handed or picturesque or sentimental. It had to feel authentic and at home in California, and especially in the Montecito hills.

Smith and the homeowners, who are longtime clients and close friends, traveled to London, Antwerp, Rome, Lisbon, and Paris, as well as New York, to locate and find the extraordinary collection of paintings, antiques, lamps, handcrafted tiles, and carpets for the estate's residence and guest quarters.

"I'm always intrigued by the romantic idea of individuality," said Smith, about gathering the estate's eclectic furniture collection. "I like each piece of furniture I design to have a very specific character and not to be mere filler."

His antiques acquisitions, selected with the owners, are grounded in more than two decades of observation, study, and constant curiosity. His purchases were driven by a deep understanding as well as a pure, passionate love of antiques and art. Smith was spurred on by the cosmopolitan Portuguese, who mixed Chinese export pottery with elaborately carved Brazilian beds in exotic woods, or Venetian paintings.

Like the finest connoisseurs, Smith has a fantastic eye for antiques and can appreciate craft and beauty and symmetry and perfection or imperfection in all its guises and forms. Like legendary dealers such as Carlton Hobbs in London, or Axel Vervoordt in Antwerp, he relishes oddity and eccentricity, and for the Montecito home his acquisitions were wide-ranging, from simple Indian cotton bedspreads or French garden chairs to a wildly rococo gilded Venetian mirror.

"I think people are often surprised to discover that I use low-key antiques a lot," he said. "The general perception is that rooms with antiques can be very formal. Nothing could be further from the truth. Rooms with a mix of country and elegant antiques are personal, comfortable, and above all individual. Carefully chosen, quality antiques give rooms character."

SMILES OF A SUMMER DAY (Opposite and Above) Guest quarters are lavished with large-scale rattan sofas and chairs, breezy painted old French garden furniture, terra-cotta tile floors, and luxurious views of tall oaks and eucalyptus all around. Here, too, Michael Smith has selected antiques—but pieces that are relaxed and easy-going. The pale color of the stucco walls was inspired by classic Portuguese quintas.

SUMMER DAY RETREAT
(Opposite and Right)
Cool white Frette bed linens as well as
French doors that open to a shaded
terrace guarantee relaxed afternoons
in July's drowsy heat. The antique
painted Venetian bedposts were found
in Venice, and custom-crafted into a
larger bed. The printed cotton curtains
are by Bennison. Throughout the
Montecito estate residence and guest
quarters, Michael Smith's consistently
cosmopolitan approach to the décor
presents a cohesive vision. In the guest
bedroom and bathroom, blue tiles,
simple curtain rods, antiques with
character, and hand-blocked textiles
bring calm, charm, and order to the
interiors. Especially important in the
guest quarters, every amenity has been
considered, including magnifying
mirrors, extra pillows, reading lamps,
light-blocking curtains, and stacks of
white towels.

The antique furniture at the quinta is not necessarily fragile or precious, said Smith.

"If an antique has stood the test of time, you can continue to use that chair, table, or desk every day," he said. "I am never afraid to mix periods and styles of antiques. Mixing antique dining chairs with a newly commissioned table, for example, gives a room personality. In the dining room of the residence, ornate rococo chairs with gilded details are juxtaposed with Chinese export pottery plates made for the Lisbon market, hung on the walls. It's just this kind of detail you would see in a Portuguese house."

The goal with every detail of the house and guest rooms was to make a weekend visit effortless, relaxing. Guests may play tennis, swim, go hiking through the grounds, read and write on the shaded terrace, play billiards in the game room, or enjoy a salad on one of the many loggias and terraces. While a trip to Summerland to go antiquing might be a wintertime pursuit, in summer guests would hardly want to leave the property all weekend.

"I love houses that are truly lived in, with family and dogs and friends around," said Smith. "Many of my clients—stars and highly accomplished people with busy lives—have children, and I know it is possible to have rooms with style that are also child- and pet-friendly. Just because you have young kids does not mean furniture has to be bulletproof. "

In the end, the project took almost three years, with the owners and Smith overseeing the minutest details, from carved mirrors and sisal carpets and footstools, to awnings, grout, gravel, faucets, kitchen tiles, carved stone mantels, and honed limestone floors, while landscape designer Mia Lehrer shaped, planted, and planned ponds, pathways, orange groves, rose arbors, and hidden bowers.

For all the talent involved, this new classic Montecito estate is simply a triumph. ■

ANGLE OF REPOSE (Above) In the Las Encinitas guest suites, the designer and the architects created rooms with elegant detailing within the cottagelike proportions of the rooms. Designer Michael Smith selected a large-scale four-poster bed, in the Portuguese Colonial style and handcarved in mahogany, for a room overlooking the gardens. In the media/game room, a dramatic gilt-framed portrait flirts from a corner beside the window, which is dressed in a striped Indian block print.

CONSISTENT VISION (Opposite) Michael Smith knows how to give decoration personality with one virtuoso piece in a room or a suite—a madly extravagant bed, a rich ruby-red chair, a grandly gilded frame, handsome curtains, or even a pillow made from a fragment of antique embroidered textile. Elegantly crafted curtains with a pattern that appears artlessly hand-blocked add contrast and pattern while appearing rather neutral; a neat trick.

ECHOES OF PORTUGAL (Opposite and Above) Everything has been created for the enjoyment and pleasure of guests. The guest quarters, separate from the main residence, are an oasis of calm and privacy, with a shaded terrace, green views, scented paths, and silence. After a few sets on the nearby tennis court, guests can gather on the terrace and meditate by the lily pond. This is bliss, indeed.

A STUDY FOR REPOSE
(Opposite and Right)
Annette Simmons decorated Piranhurst to look as if it had never changed. Carved stone fireplaces, original to the house, hold pride of place. The actor Gene Hackman, who was the previous owner, hired Palm Springs designer Steve Chase to give the interiors a Palm Desert spin, complete with grass-cloth walls, heavy window coverings, plantation shutters on the windows, and contemporary furniture, Simmons noted. She traveled to Paris and London to find antiques and made friends among the antiques dealers in Summerland, where she made many significant purchases, including Florentine desks, antique Italian armoires, and elegant Italianate tables.

MONTECITO HERITAGE

WITH GRANDEUR, GRACE, a sunny outlook, and superbly maintained rose gardens, the elegant and historic Piranhurst estate dances into new decades.

Gilt-edged San Franciscans make walk-on appearances and many starring roles in the early-twentieth-century history of the Santa Barbara area and especially in the creation of the great estates of Montecito.

These Nob Hill and Russian Hill grandees, with their East Coast educations, pockets full of Gold Rush gold, advantageous multiple marriages, and impressive fortunes from railroads, banking, real estate development, water, even coffee, were attracted to year-round golden weather and to the assured summer sunshine and shimmering beaches lacking in northern California.

Their friends, business associates, and fellow private club members, polo players, and cultural philanthropists had been among pioneers in the region, so it was only natural that a second or third residence in southern California would become fashionable, and perhaps truly

necessary, given San Francisco's notoriously chilly and foggy August weather.

Henry Bothin, one of the largest landowners in San Francisco at the turn of the century, built Piranhurst in 1917 for his young second wife, Ellen Chabot. She was the daughter of wealthy Anthony Chabot, who in the late nineteenth century dammed the waters of San Leandro Creek east of Oakland, created a vast reservoir, and set up the first private water system bringing water to the East Bay.

Ellen Chabot had equally creative and grandiose visions for Piranhurst, eventually building a hilltop tea garden (with an elaborate watering system) and pavilion high above the residence.

Piranhurst takes its name from St. Piran, a fifth-century Irish saint who eventually made his way to

Cornwall, where legend holds that he discovered tin. Thus he became the patron saint of tin miners—such as, centuries later, Henry Bothin. (Bothin, like many northern California investors, made a fortune from mining.)

Bothin's history (and fortune) was rather typical of his San Francisco and Santa Barbara friends. He had migrated from the Midwest to San Francisco and had made his first fortune in gold, coffee, and spices by 1875. With his profits, he bought vast tracts of land in San Francisco, still in its infancy after the Gold Rush, and he owned commercial real estate in downtown San Francisco at the time of the Great Earthquake in 1906.

Bothin and his wife loved to entertain at Piranhurst, and their parties were attended by social figures from Montecito, as well as San Francisco.

Almost eighty years later, it was the fate of Texans Annette and Harold Simmons and their considerable fortune to revive Piranhurst, which over the decades had become a sleeping beauty. The couple, who live in Dallas, have spent the last eighteen years restoring and redecorating Piranhurst, and now spend as much of the year as possible in Montecito. They make lengthy sojourns in the summer to escape the Dallas heat and humidity.

Simmons, a native Texan like his wife, is one of a handful of self-made American billionaires, but started life as the dirt-poor son of rural east Texas schoolteachers. (He has been known to joke about his humble beginnings to the Simmons'

CALLIGRAPHY OF TREES
(Left) A mile-long driveway lined
with palm trees and noble
California oaks leads up the hill
to the iron gates, the entry
courtyard, and parklike gardens
of Piranhurst. Walls are
covered—as they have been since
1917—with trimmed and clipped
Ficus Pumila vines. Box hedges
add their own sculptural
elegance. A stream and tennis
courts are hidden beyond the
palm trees and oaks, adding to
the Arcadian vision of the estate.

neighbor, Oprah, who visits to check on Annette's rose gardens, which have been featured on her television show.) Simmons, a financier, now controls many companies, including corporations listed on the New York Stock Exchange.

With donations to Texas universities, medical centers, Dallas charities, and one of the largest gifts for medical research in the United States, Simmons, in his seventies, seems energized by making money and giving it away. The couple also takes particular pride in the upkeep of Piranhurst.

Today, the Simmons family employs four full-time gardeners to tend their trees, groom the lawns, trim the topiaries and hedges, keep urns of geraniums and petunias flourishing, and ensure that the many citrus trees are well fed and happy. A specialist rosarian on staff is assigned to take care of all the roses.

Annette Simmons consulted with Santa Barbara master rosarian Dan Bifano before selecting her hundreds of roses.

"Oprah loves to visit my rose gardens, and we always swap notes," said Annette. "She says my roses are the best and biggest in Montecito, but I love the glorious and beautiful colors of her roses. Dan Bifano takes care of our roses, and he makes sure they are all 'flower-show ready' for nine months of the year."

Among the rose selections Simmons made with Bifano: "Barbra Streisand" (the singer, a rose collector, is also a neighbor), "Chris Evert," "Marilyn Monroe," "Iceberg," "Sunset Celebration," "Yves Piaget," "Mr. Lincoln," and Oprah's new "Legends" rose.

"The rose gardens are my favorite pursuit at Piranhurst," said Annette. "I can spend hours tending them and enjoying them. In Montecito, everything flourishes." ∎

ESTATE OF GRACE
(Opposite) Like the flawless Palladian villas in Italy that were vivid inspirations for this Montecito villa, El Eliseo has the extra flourish of an elegant swath of swimming pool, visible from the windows of the residence. From upper floors, the Channel Islands can be seen after early morning fog burns off.

(Right) Even the entry to the pool house has been graced with elegant architectural details. On the arched over-door, an annunciation scene is played out with winged angels and floral motifs in delicately molded terra cotta. It is original to the 1919 house.

NOW, VOYAGER

AT HER MAJESTIC MONTECITO VILLA, El Eliseo, intrepid traveler Virginia Castagnola Hunter tends her prized apricot and pink roses and rare species of palms before wild places of the world call her once more.

One glance at the splendor of the glamorous villa, its glorious acres of sheltered gardens, languid pools, splashing fountains, and dramatic ocean views, and any visitor must wonder why Montecito arts philanthropist Virginia Castagnola Hunter would ever leave El Eliseo—or spend much of her time traveling to the far corners of the earth.

Her residence, one of the beauties in the heart of Montecito, was built in 1919 by architect Reginald Johnson, who finessed a superbly delineated classic Italian villa. Johnson was the architect of the 1927

Biltmore Hotel, also an ode to Mediterranean languor, with its arcades, courtyards, and elegant bougainvillea-swathed private gardens.

Johnson, like other early Santa Barbara region architects, freely sampled concepts from the historic architecture of Tuscany, the Veneto, Andalusia, Morocco, and other classic Mediterranean styles. After completing El Eliseo, Johnson created Lotusland, the thirty-seven-acre estate that Polish opera singer Ganna Walska turned into her own enduring fantasy of moon gardens and blue agave groves.

Hunter and her husband, Kenneth Hume Hunter Jr., acquired a rather disheveled El Eliseo in the 1970s. (The name refers to the Elysian Fields, home of the blessed in Greek mythology.)

"Reginald Johnson was a genius at siting houses," said Hunter. "In the morning I wake up and see the early-morning light on the ocean. Every moment of the day, rooms are flooded with light. The sunlight blesses you and cheers you."

Hunter is a member of the Travelers' Century Club (membership requires that travelers have visited a hundred countries), and in her life of adventure she has visited more than three hundred territories, countries, islands, archipelagos, and dependencies and every ocean, sea, and islet.

In any given month, she is likely to be returning from Lakshadweep, in the Arabian Sea, or heading for Iwo Jima, in the Pacific Ocean, or to Tristan da Cunha, the most remote island in the world, a green mirage in the southern Atlantic.

"I got the travel bug when I was in high school, and my parents sent me to Europe for one of the classic study tours," recalled Hunter. That fateful summer, she notched up twenty countries. Name a remote country or island—

MEMORIES OF RAJASTHAN
(Left) A painting of a Jodhpur
cityscape hangs on the study wall
above the single modern sofa.

THE TRAVELER'S RETURN
(Opposite) The living room was
painted several tones of coral,
with guidance from Guy Roop, a
Santa Barbara interior designer
who was also the author of a
volume on Palladio. The coral-
persimmon tones are authentic to
villas in the Veneto that inspired
the architecture and interiors of
the house. At Christmas time,
Hunter keeps a cheerful fire
burning. The carved stone
fireplace, original to the house,
was acquired in Italy and has
lotus motifs throughout its
baroque pattern. The painting is
by Yasu Eguchi. Every piece of
lumber used to construct the
house was brought by railroad
from Minnesota, where the
original homeowners grew
timber. Throughout the house are
sculptures, carpets, paintings,
textiles and objects collected
during travels.

Yemen, Zanzibar, Mongolia, Irian Jaya, the Marquesas, Tokelau—and Virginia Hunter has stopped by.

"I always wanted to experience the whole world," said Hunter, who is also a member of the Club International des Grands Voyageurs, based in Tunisia, and the Circumnavigators Club, a New York City group.

"Travel is my lifelong passion," said Hunter, whose grandparents arrived in Santa Barbara from Switzerland and Italy at the turn of the twentieth century. "I want to see everything in the world. And always I'm happy to return home."

She is soon swept up in the numerous arts causes she supports, and the legendary beauty spends hours in the garden with her gardener, checking on the agapanthus and lilies, and sizing up her olive and sycamore trees.

"This house has given my family great pleasure," said Hunter. "Every day I thank Reginald Johnson for his inspired architecture." ■

IN MONTECITO, *LA DOLCE VITA*

DESIGNER MICHAEL S. SMITH perfected the atmospheric interiors of a Tuscan-influenced house high in the hills of Montecito. Don Nulty orchestrated the evocative architecture. There's delight in every corner.

A love of Italian architecture and artistry and the seduction of princely Tuscan country houses inspired one of Montecito's newest estates, which is a tribute both to a family's quest for a poetic interpretation of authentic Tuscan style and to the local artisans and talent who made it happen.

Venetian plaster walls, handcrafted stone balustrades, hand-scraped walnut floors, and an Italianate palette of sepia, Giotto blue, and sage green all conjure up the natural richness of the Italian countryside and exude a confident and lyrical connection to the noted houses and gardens of Montecito, many of them also inspired by an admiration of Tuscan villas and Florentine palazzi.

The philanthropic couple who commissioned the house entertains with grace and generosity. They wanted a residence with private outdoor terraces and secluded courtyards, as well as grand rooms that offer both welcoming places for social gatherings and spots for quiet moments of relaxation and privacy.

"This is the kind of house I love to work on because the rooms are large and airy and quite relaxed, just like Florentine country houses," said Los Angeles interior designer Michael S. Smith, who worked on the house for two years.

In tune with his clients, he added luxurious yet understated details, like a Gregorius/Pineo four-poster

ebony bed, custom hand-printed Le Gracieux linens, curtains of cream-striped linens from his Jasper collection, and exotic nineteenth-century Anglo-Indian pearl-inlaid tables. Rare Tabriz and Mahal carpets are placed on practical sisal rugs with a subtle tape binding.

Intricate beamed and hand-plastered ceilings soar as high as fourteen feet. View-catching arched windows and doorways and luxurious stretches of terra-cotta-floored hallways provide a pitch-perfect setting.

It was important at the same time to bring down these gracious volumes to a more intimate scale with painted borders on the plaster walls, a series of large-scale Italian and French chandeliers from Europa in Summerland, down-filled sofas upholstered in subtle printed velvet, and linen curtains that hang from hand-forged iron rods to look rich but not fussy, said the

designer. For the master bedroom, an antique Tabriz carpet in faded blue and gold tones adds a splash of traditional Persian patterns to the neutral, earthy color scheme.

Smith created the distinctive mix of refined country antiques, venerable Chinese porcelains, Roman-influenced stone urns, gold-framed mirrors, Delft vases that recall Vermeer, gold-embossed Piedmontese leather screens, and velvet and damask textiles that are the signature of worldly villas in Tuscany—where they usually have been in the family for centuries.

For the large living room, Smith's trophy was a handsome ten-foot-tall seventeenth-century Tuscan *armadio* from Europa in Summerland. It was originally used for storing a patrician family's weapons and armor. Contrasting a massive seventeenth-century Italian

DINING IN SEPIA
(Opposite and Right) In the
dining room, walls were hand-
finished in rich Venetian plaster,
with delicately painted sepia
landscapes to add depth and
poetry. The blue and cream linen
fabric on the neoclassical chairs
is in perfect harmony with a
graphic collection of Chinese
temple jars and Delft urns and
platters. The eighteenth-century
Italian walnut credenza has its
original hardware. The giltwood
sconces were designed by
Michael Smith.

walnut bibliotheca with a pair of graceful late-nineteenth-century gilt-framed Venetian mirrors, he also added the allure of a colorful antique Chinese cloisonné lamp and a massive Tuscan baroque credenza, from around 1720, with its original iron locks, keys, and drawer hardware—all of which played against a series of graceful gilded sconces of his own design.

Smith does not aim for museumlike authenticity and avoids theme design. Staying true to a Tuscan mood and with a knowing sense of centuries of Italian adventurers and explorers (designers owe a debt to Marco Polo), he selected a bold pair of blue and white Chinese porcelain temple jars, along with antique Chinese export vases and Delft bowls that add a cosmopolitan air to the rooms.

The new décor looks as if it has evolved over decades, not months. The feeling of the rooms is airy and comfortable, with rich and textured handwoven silks, and superb craftsmanship everywhere expressed on every surface. But nothing is obvious. It doesn't scream luxury or opulence.

Over almost two decades, Smith has built a career on coherent interiors influenced and guided by historic design. He offers the authenticity and grace of the original interiors (French, English, Italian, Belgian, or Hollywood Regency) with a knowing twist, rich and timeless classicism, and a contemporary air. Fluent in many design vocabularies, he can conjure up a light-hearted Portuguese quinta in Santa Ynez, the style of an English manor in Beverly Hills, or the relaxed chic of an Antwerp loft in Malibu. ■

ARCH RIVALS (Opposite and Left) Architect Don Nulty is also a knowledgeable architecture historian. Bold, handsome—and historically correct—arches welcome the family home from travels.

THE MASTER BEDROOM suite displays Michael Smith's superbly controlled color palette of diffused cream and ivory tones punched up with variations of blues and pale green. The bravura bed, inspired by the heritage of Tuscan craftsmanship, is by Gregorius Pineo.

CHAPTER TWO
GLORIOUS GARDENS

A perpetual summer and south-facing plateaus poised on the Pacific Ocean afford the Santa Barbara region an ideal climate for lavish gardens. Horticulture here is an art and an avocation. American landmark landscapes flourish in this setting.

THE TRIUMPH OF ETERNAL BEAUTY

LAS TEJAS IN MONTECITO, a national horticultural treasure, was inspired by the formality, architecture, and lush sensuality of Italian Renaissance gardens.

Las Tejas, in the heart of Montecito, began with a dream of the timeless glories of formal Italian gardens that graced the historic palazzi and villas of Rome and Florence.

Helen Seymour Stafford Thorne, the chatelaine of Las Tejas from 1917 to 1941, was the highly accomplished landscape designer who created the majestic acres of lily ponds, reflecting pools, clipped hedges, pavilions, and statuary. The hilltop villa and garden offer views of the cypress-framed ocean and Channel Islands glimmering in the misty blue haze at the horizon.

Thorne, the wife of Oakleigh Lewis Thorne, traveled extensively to view the most significant gardens of Italy. Thorne has created her own horticultural version of the Grand Tour, taking a surveyor's interest in the architectural plans of each villa garden, noting the strongly structured axes, the water-conserving plantings, and the allées of clipped yews with the punctuation of fountains and belvederes for viewpoints.

The Las Tejas garden was said to have been inspired by the dramatic and singular gardens of Villa Farnese, built near Viterbo by Giacomo da Vignola in 1559. (The noble villa and garden, a few hours north of Rome, are still open for viewing, and are among the most historically significant in Italy.) However, the two gardens are not at all alike.

While Villa Farnese no doubt offered her inspiration, it is more likely that Thorne refined and defined her concept of garden architecture through the study of a series of villas and landscapes. Many princely estates in Italy, like Las Tejas, were built on hilltops with gardens cascading down toward distant horizons.

Thorne's concept of strong axial views, formally shaped hedges and lawns, and a reliance on structure rather than the seasonal flourish of colorful flowers, was clearly inspired by her extensive travels through the great Renaissance villa and palazzo gardens of Italy. Hers is a

A SENSE OF FORMALITY (Opposite and Right) Scrolls of hand-clipped box lead the eye down the hillside toward the Italian Renaissance–style temple that punctuates the vista. At left, a series of Romanesque columns support a wisteria pergola. Agave plants in stone urns on classical plinths add a sense of movement to the carefully composed formal landscape.

garden for all seasons, relying on clipped ivy, carpets of lawn, tall cypress, and agave for year-round green vistas.

Oakleigh and Helen Thorne arrived in Montecito in 1917 from Millbrook, in Dutchess County, New York, and soon acquired the twenty-six-acre property. Mrs. Thorne could see beyond the rather ordinary adobe residence with its tiled roof (*las tejas* is Spanish for "roof tiles") and traditional Spanish interior courtyard. She had a vision for the hillside gardens.

Her work began with the same formal planting as classic Florentine gardens. She relied on the crisp delineation of pathways, hedges, clipped box, and topiaries to create poetic harmony, with wisteria pergolas, garden rooms with walls of Eugenia and yew, for added delight.

With her plans in hand—and a team of talented gardeners—she created one of the masterpieces of landscape design in the United States.

In the 1920s the Thornes engaged architect George Washington Smith to turn the adobe house into a gracious villa befitting the garden.

In 1941, alarmed by early signs of war, the Thornes sold their estate for $40,000. Over the next sixty years the residence changed hands several times, and while the house was intermittently updated, repaired, and restored with care and devotion by conservation specialists, the garden was allowed to fall into ruin.

Today, the illustrious property is in the hands of philanthropists Peter and Stephanie Sperling, who spent eight years diligently and creatively working on an extensive restoration of the garden. Using historical records from the Smithsonian, they began a bold program of restoring it to its original state. Statuary was repaired, hardscape was restored, and protective redwoods, ancient oaks, and sycamores were groomed and nurtured.

The landscape and the estate are responsibly managed with the environment in mind: it is free of pesticides, and beneficial insects, birds, and other fauna are actively encouraged. Almost a century after Helen Thorne created her dream garden, Las Tejas is once more in full glory. ■

GARDEN FANTASIES (Above, Opposite, and Following Pages) The large acreage of Las Tejas has allowed a series of owners to create their own horticultural dreams. While the style and structure of the gardens are Italian Renaissance in direction, in side gardens secluded among verdure and in quiet corners of the estate, there are a Japanese garden, a vine-covered arbor (an ideal location for a dreamy spring luncheon), and noble marble statuary hidden behind hedges.

FANTASY ISLAND (Opposite) The house, inspired by a Caribbean Colonial–style house (itself designed to suggest Cuba) on a film set in Los Angeles, is nestled among sixty acres of privacy and is virtually surrounded by water. Grass-edged streams and koi ponds surround the palm-punctuated gardens and rooms on all sides. Scented ginger plants, along with vibrant canna lilies, papyrus, pampas grass, trumpet vines, and New Zealand flax, thrive in the shelter of centuries-old California live oaks. Tall gates enclose the property, which is hidden in a canyon. "Tropical plants do well here, as we are very protected and Santa Barbara seldom experiences a frost," noted Webb.

(Right) Martha, an inquisitive East African Crowned Crane, is one of the members of Webb's exotic aviary.

BIRDS IN PARADISE

IN A HIDDEN CANYON near Santa Barbara, legendary designer Bobby Webb and his partner, Michael Corbett, retreat to their private world of tropical birds, fragrant plants, and transcendent peace.

For the last three decades, Bobby Webb has been a designer and builder of legendary and luxurious Santa Barbara–area estates. Were he to offer a tour of the best addresses of Montecito and beyond, he can indicate the grand iron-gated entrances to the hilltop mansion of Oprah's friends and neighbors, a rustic hacienda hidden among oaks, a polo pony stable, and gardens on the former Armour Estate, now the residence of a noted (and highly successful) Hollywood producer-director. There is also the Addison Mizener–style villa Webb and his brother, Joey, also a designer, conceived and planned, with its dramatic motor court and sunken Roman-style pool.

"I create total environments for my clients, always grand in scale, including the residence, the landscape, guest quarters, pools, and everything down to the custom-made hardware," said Webb.

And so it was not surprising that a few years ago the self-described "hysterical, hyper" Webb set about designing his own Santa Barbara refuge for himself and his longtime partner, Michael Corbett—and the toucans, flamingos, and koi that he loves and collects.

His site is a steep sixty-acre canyon, hidden from sight and tranquil but within easy driving distance from downtown Santa Barbara.

The Caribbean Colonial—style house Webb created was, he recalled, inspired by a movie set at Universal Studios, built to be a stand-in for a Cuban plantation residence. Webb designed it with his brother, Joey, with whom he often collaborates.

Bobby Webb and Michael Corbett haunted the antiques shops in Summerland, just down the coast. Summerhill Antiques and Lifestyles Antiques offered up the signature mix of Italian Renaissance—style chairs, Chinese tables, antique English bamboo armchairs, and vivid Chinese pottery vases and urns. But there's nothing precious here. Webb's goal was a relaxed atmosphere, a suggestion of tropical languor. Mission accomplished. ■

BIRDS OF A FEATHER (Above) Webb created a harmonious habitat for his exotic birds, including ponds for his corps de ballet of flamingoes. Also among his tropical avian menagerie are macaws, toucans, and hornbills, all well protected and housed in a custom-built aviary that is partially shaded by a profusion of palms and oaks.

MASTER OF AESTHETICS (Opposite) Taking his cue from classic Caribbean Colonial plantation outposts, Webb gave the house an eighteenth-century air, complete with traceries of fretwork, elaborate staircases, a practical metal roof, and broad shady verandas.

THE GRACE OF AN ENGLISH GARDEN

ROB AND SHERYL LOWE celebrated the classic elegance of heavily scented old-fashioned roses in their Santa Barbara garden.

When Rob and Sheryl Lowe acquired their hillside property, which included six acres of orange groves surrounding a would-be French chateau and overgrown olive trees, Sheryl knew precisely the new design direction she wanted to create for the residence and the garden.

The former film-industry makeup artist and her actor husband, Rob, had lived for several months on a country estate in North Wales while Rob was working on a lengthy film project there. Sheryl photographed the superbly maintained estate gardens. She also researched, visited, and gathered her own files of England's finest country gardens. She had fallen in love with their characteristic pastel clouds of old-fashioned roses, their lush seasonal plantings, and their subtle colors that seemed to duplicate Impressionist paintings.

Sheryl's concept for the Santa Barbara site was to create a formal plan that would be the framework for creative and artistic English-style planting. Her concept of an English garden was taken from a long history of beauty and inspiration going back several hundred years. With the help of local landscape designer Sandra Devine and landscaper Jim Boysel, Sheryl brought in fully grown trees for shelter and structure. Garden guru

ROSE IS A ROSE
(Opposite and Right)
One of the great pleasures of
growing beautiful and fragrant
roses such as "Yves Piaget," which
thrives in the Santa Barbara
climate, is cutting the flowers in
the early morning, arranging them
simply, and placing them indoors
for all to enjoy. Sheryl Lowe's
conservatory serves as her cutting
room, which she has decorated
with botanical paintings, practical
baskets, terra-cotta pots, and chic
sconces—as well as chairs and
tables where she can entertain.

Thomas Cole nurtured and managed the vegetable gardens and fruit trees.

The history of English garden design is jeweled with the names of talented landscape designers such as William Kent, "Capability" Brown, and Humphrey Repton, who all left their mark with classical landscapes that still exist.

English gardens and estates had been rather formal until in the 1890s the highly influential English landscape designer Gertrude Jekyll applied her informal concepts of cottage garden plantings around structured garden layouts and architecture. Her book, *Color in the Flower Garden* (1908), is still in print, and has become the English gardener's bible.

In the Lowes' garden, color harmonies, such as the painterly pinks of "Yves Piaget" roses, were intermingled with drifts of white geranium varieties, all carefully contrived to look natural. Hellebores and *Alchemilla Mollis* were planted along paths, and in Jekyll's (and the Lowes') world, plants grow naturally in a very pleasing jumble, with flowering shrubs and hardy perennials mingled with delectably fragrant roses.

In the Lowes' garden (which has been featured on Oprah Winfrey's television show), clematis and roses clamber up trees and over bowers, arches, trellises, and pergolas. Sun-loving and drought-resistant *Stachys byzantina* (lamb's ear) plants add their woolly leaves to the bouquet. Roses wreathe windows, and hydrangeas tumble across paths beneath trees. Just as in English gardens, delphiniums, foxgloves, and aquilegias grow right up to the doorway. Seedlings are planted informally, coming up as if they had sown themselves or been blown by the wind.

The Lowes' borders were planted with many of Jekyll's favorite flowering perennials in a kind of controlled chaos. Arranged artfully but loosely around a conservatory and along paths in subtle color palettes and in interwoven drifts are flowers including hollyhocks, penstemon, rosemary and lavender, nicotiana, bergenias, artemisia, and nepeta, as well as peonies and handsome Japanese anemones, which all complement and frame the selection of roses.

Just as in the classic English cottage garden, there is an enclosed garden with a rose and jasmine arbor, hollyhocks, and delphinium, all of them favorite nineteenth-century flowers. The Lowes' garden emphasized authenticity, with old-fashioned roses that bloomed once a year with rich scents, and simple flowers, fragrant lavender, and herbs such as verbena, sage, and lavender that add to the harmonious feeling.

The Lowes also commissioned Santa Barbara architect Don Nulty to build a new house, as well as a guest house, and added a rich green lawn as a sports field for their two young sons.

This is a garden where hidden paths lead down a hillside to a creek-side space planted with a selection of native plants, and an in-season swimming hole, plus a mossy clearing beneath old oak trees.

But it's the English garden that impresses.

William Kent, the great nineteenth-century English garden designer, who began his career as a painter and taught himself architecture in Rome, believed that "All gardening is a landscape painting." He would love the Lowes' garden, which is a tribute to Gertrude Jekyll and, with its pastel palette, to Monet at Giverny, and most of all to Sheryl Lowe's vision of paradise. ■

CHAPTER THREE
PRIVATE LIVES

The tradition of grand dreams and unlimited aspirations has set the tone for the pursuit of personal style and happiness in the hills of Montecito and Santa Barbara. Expressive interiors, "a reverie on possibilities," make their home among superbly tended gardens.

WELCOME AND FAREWELL
(Right) Montecito interior designer Penny Bianchi's entry gate shows the artistry of Bruce Rapf, who created magic with the trimmings from the family's willow tree. Rapf also designed the Bianchis' water gardens.

MEDITERRANEAN DREAMS
(Opposite) Penny Bianchi furnished the loggia, which overlooks the garden and the pond, with slightly faded vintage wicker chairs and a sofa, as well as a pleasantly knocked-about antique Italian walnut table, and a pair of unmatched Italian glazed white terra cotta garden stools in the form of tasseled pillows. In the left corner is an antique Italian ceramic stove, which the family uses for illumination and warmth on cool winter evenings. Radiant heat was installed beneath the Saltillo floor tiles so that the family can enjoy cocktails or tea there even when the winter rains are pouring down. The drifting curtains were made from antique French monogrammed linen bed sheets. In this living theater, ivy and Virginia creeper are welcomed inside.

UNE MAISON ROMANTIQUE

IN MONTECITO, Adam and Penny Bianchi created their own pleasure pavilion, complete with a nature habitat alive with birdsong.

Montecito interior designer Penny Bianchi grew up in Pasadena, and decided to move to Montecito ten years ago with her husband, Adam.

"We had visited Montecito on our honeymoon, thirty years ago, and had always longed to live here someday," recalled Penny Bianchi. "We came to find our dream house."

The Bianchis admire old, atmospheric houses and were haunted by the relaxed grace of the classic residence they'd lived in happily in Pasadena.

"We wanted a house with history—a house with a feeling of a life well lived—and we simply could not find one in Montecito that was right," said Penny. "We looked at about fifty houses, always setting off with great optimism and hope. Nothing turned up."

"Old" was not the only key criterion.

"I'm an animal lover, and my agenda was to secure a property where we could raise rare chickens and nurture our rescued corgis and cats, and where we would attract

INTERNATIONAL PALETTE
(Below and Left) Decorator Penny Bianchi scoured consignment shops—and the auction of the estate of Tony Duquette—for her porcelain collections that include a pair of handsome Veronese green parrots. The eighteenth-century *Famille rose* and *Famille verte* Chinese porcelains were a gift from her mother, who lived in Shanghai in the twenties. Collections are displayed throughout the house, always artfully styled to appear artless and never standing on ceremony. Dust, plentiful here beneath the old oak trees, is an essential element for the relaxed mood.

COMPANIONABLE COLLECTIONS
(Opposite) In the living room, a neoclassical stone mantel was found in London. The leopard-skin-covered stool dates from the twenties, and paisley textiles used on the armchairs are nineteenth-century Kashmiri shawls Bianchi purchased at a Paris flea market.

native birds and hummingbirds with nectar-filled flowers," Bianchi said.

Finally, after looking at fifty properties, Bianchi and her Realtor took an informal visit to a two-and-a-half-acre site circled by ninety acres of nature preserves and a large private estate.

"My Realtor told me there were coyotes, bobcats, deer, and raccoons in the adjacent nature preserves surrounding the land," said Bianchi. Also nearby, and visible from the property, is the largest sequoia grove on private property in the United States.

"Those noble sequoias and specimen palm trees are my borrowed landscape," said the designer.

As it turned out, the site was not on the market. Daring to hope, the Bianchis made an offer to the owner—and were given a swift ultimatum: decide in two hours and the price would be halved.

"It was an offer we could not refuse," said Adam, who is Penny's business manager. Sold!

For their new residence, the Bianchis sought to duplicate the practical interiors of an eighteenth-century French pavilion, with a large central living room/dining room, and just one luxurious bedroom. It would be a glorious small house with a five-hundred-square-foot loggia overlooking the gardens. A willow grove and a lily pond, lush and green and very Monet-at-Giverny, were added.

"I wanted the house, from the start, to look as if it had been there for decades," said Bianchi.

The moment the contractors departed, she planted one hundred and fifty Virginia creeper plants around the perimeter of the house. They now curtain the walls.

Both the plaster interior walls and the stucco exterior walls were tinted and coated with pink-tinged ocher

THE FRENCH IDEAL (Above) Penny Bianchi often travels to France, and it was on one of her excursions that she found the antique copper bath that she installed in her sunny bathroom. The windows overlook a private, enclosed garden. A bamboo pagoda was turned into an artful light fixture, another Tony Duquette inspiration.

HOUSE OF DREAMS (Opposite) Penny Bianchi's art is to create new interiors that look as if they've been in the family for generations. In this guest bedroom, walls were plastered to appear faded and time-tempered, and her charming fabrics were selected to look as if they had been collected over many decades of flea market searches.

pigments from Roussillon in the south of France. Over time a lime wash and the integral earth colors have resulted in walls that are richly mottled with a translucent, chalky patina that seems to have weathered centuries.

"I wanted to make the property a nature preserve, so I called the National Wildlife Federation for advice," recalled Bianchi. "They sent me lists of plants, and invaluable tips about fountains and ponds, as well as native plants to attract butterflies and birds."

In the dark of night, from January to August, small native tree frogs chirp and splash in the pond. Chickadees and warblers flit around the house and accompany breakfast on the loggia with their distinctive cheery banter. Butterflies sun themselves on flat rocks around the pond carpeted with glossy lily pads.

Kingfishers chatter in the oak trees, blue herons squawk as they stalk through the rushes, and spotted Belgian Mille Fleur d'Uccles bantams cackle behind the hedge.

For the interiors, Penny Bianchi had only to unpack her lifetime of French and Italian antiques, paintings by Marcel Vertès, and her Chinese porcelains, tole auriculas in tiny pots, Turkish carpets, Kashmiri paisley shawls, and Moroccan and Romanian antique textiles bought in Paris.

"I never thought I would love this house so much, but it is captivating every season and every moment of the day," said Bianchi.

The corgis are vigilant companions. The air is fragrant with the vibrant scents of citrus blossoms and eucalyptus.

"It's intoxicating," said Bianchi. ■

GARDEN PARTY
(Opposite and Right)
John Saladino cultivated a
Mediterranean-style, drought-
tolerant garden with a subtle
color palette and year-round
beauty. His secret garden, in the
shade of mature olive trees,
centers on a nine-hundred-year-
old Chinese gristmill stone posed
on a new stone pedestal to serve
as a welcoming table. The
practical folding teak chairs are a
longtime Saladino favorite. On
the terrace, which has views of
the Montecito hills and the
harbor in the distance, Saladino
sets out comfortable seating and
pillows. On summer afternoons,
garden umbrellas are moved into
place to provide shade and a slice
of coolness.

A DESIGNER'S MOMENT IN THE SUN

JOHN SALADINO'S modern house in Montecito offers brilliant lessons in subtle nature-inspired colors and the art of the elegant mix.

Visionary New York architect and interior designer John Saladino acquired his first house in Santa Barbara in 1987: an elegant music pavilion on a historic estate (it is now owned by Oprah Winfrey). The music pavilion was an all-too-brief stay for Saladino, who was soon in need of a new Montecito perch. After leaving his first romantic house, the requirement for his second one was rushed by the arrival of an East Coast blizzard. During a particularly harsh winter at his country house in Connecticut, Saladino called a realtor in Santa Barbara and urgently asked her to find a small house with a great view. He wanted to get serious about a purchase, fast.

"I arrived in Montecito, and we walked onto the hillside property, and I immediately saw the magnificent panorama of the harbor, the hills, the mountains, and I said, 'I'll take it,'" recalled the designer. "I then walked inside the house, which was modern in its architectural approach. I knew I could make it work."

So impatient was Saladino to luxuriate in the sunshine that he repaired the house, painted it, installed the art and furniture, arranged and furnished terraces, and started replanting the landscape—all in three weeks.

The stucco exterior was painted a pale sandalwood tone, inspired by the eucalyptus trees that are so abundant on his property. Rosemary, jasmine, lavender, and several varieties of solanum plants, along with silver-gray olive trees and Portuguese cork oaks that surround the house, provided him with the color scheme for the interior, with its lavender-blue linen slipcovers, taupe linen upholstery, quilted white linen tablecloths, and lilac-color taffeta wall hangings. The floors were covered in practical Saltillo tiles.

STUDYING THE CLASSICS
(Opposite and Right)
The pared-down architecture of the living room, with its pale sand-colored walls stripped of detail, offer the brilliant Saladino a stage for creating and shaping vignettes that constantly entertain the eye. With etchings of old Santa Barbara propped in a casual manner on the mantel, a television (the electronic fireplace) alongside the fireplace, and comfortable chairs in companionable and conversational arrangements, the room is prepared for every occasion. Also in the living room, a California plein-air painting leans on a Flemish tooled leather occasional chair, beside a ziggurat of antique Chinese lacquered tables backed by a periwinkle- blue linen sofa.

THE ART OF ARRANGEMENT (Opposite and Above) Saladino can take a modern room with simple pale putty-colored walls and turn it into a rich feast of visual delights. He dressed a pair of chairs of his own design with pale blue Fortuny fabric accented with grosgrain tape, and sharpened things up with crisp striped silk cushions. The quilted silk wall hanging, a favorite Saladino device, offers a frame for an antique Italian chest lavished with gleaming silver trays, and a grand silver pitcher revealed by a splash of turquoise pottery. The pair of antique terra-cotta English lions on plain white plinths neatly guard a pair of speakers set into the wall.

Summer on the hillside turned the house into a sun-trap, so Saladino craned in several more large Portuguese cork oaks to add shade to the house. Well schooled in East Coast landscape design, he turned his green thumb to planting for a hot, dry, Mediterranean-style climate. The original landscape included whispering eucalyptus trees, pine trees, and woody native creosote bushes. He amended the stony soil and set up watering systems. *Verbena bonariensis*, *Solanum crispum*, *Solanum jasminoides,* santolina, and star jasmine, for night fragrance, turned the garden into the Amalfi coast.

"I planted the new shrubs and plants in a casual style to look as if they had been broadcast by birds," said the designer.

Saladino had had a lifelong dream of living in California. He first arrived in Santa Barbara at the age of sixteen, on a family holiday, and had a *coup de foudre* that hadn't dimmed in forty years.

"We stayed at the Biltmore Hotel, and for me, from the Midwest, it was like an apparition, with the ocean, the mountains, the intoxicating smell of salt air and eucalyptus," said the designer. "I already knew I was going to be an architect and designer. And I knew I would eventually live in Santa Barbara."

Saladino, originally from Kansas City, went on to graduate from Notre Dame and the Yale School of Art and Architecture. After working in Rome with architect Piero Sartogo, he returned to New York in 1972 to open his own design practice, Saladino Group, Inc., an architectural and interior design organization with a staff of thirty.

The Montecito house became his design inspiration, his refuge, his winter respite, and a retreat when he had major projects. With his West Coast outpost, he also attracted California clients.

"In my design, I edit to the point of creating the maximum effect," said Saladino. "In a garden, I would plant one beautiful flower or plant, or four hundred tulips or lilies—nothing in between. For the same reason—that the middle ground is seldom of great interest or beauty—I like Gap jeans or Giorgio Armani menswear, but nothing in between." ∎

POLLEN GRAINS FROM A
DISTANT STAR
(Opposite and Right)
The Shannons planted three different varieties of lavender in their gardens, including deep purple *Lavandula angustifolia* (classic English lavender), dark violet *Lavandula dentata* (traditional French lavender), and *Lavandula x intermedia* "Provence," the fragrant lavender plant grown in fields all over Provence. The lavender plants, all eight hundred of them, stay in bloom most of the year in the balmy temperatures at nine hundred feet above sea level. The three cultivars thrive on their sunny hilltop and in the afternoon flood the house with their sweet and drowsy scent. The Shannons designed the earthy, pale ochre integral-color stucco and lime wash on the exterior of the house so that it would look centuries old. The concept was to make the house look and feel rustic—not new.

PERFUMED EVIDENCE OF HAPPINESS

DIZZY WITH LOVE of Provence, Travis and Tracy Shannon dreamed up their ode to all things Provençal on a seven-acre estate near Santa Barbara.

Travis and Tracy Shannon, who both grew up in Santa Barbara, went on vacation to France six years ago and fell head over heels in love with the wild backcountry of Provence. With their two young children they explored the winding streets of historic villages, visited the hill towns, and drove among fields of lavender, taking in the character and peace of the region.

At La Bastide de Moustiers, the Shannon family's favorite place to enjoy the summer holidays, chef Alain Ducasse and French interior designer Tonia Peyrot distilled the essence of timeless Provençal design to create a warm country inn that was utterly casual, with hammocks beneath the trees in the garden, but with Michelin-starred dining at the end of a sunstruck day.

Peyrot's décor at La Bastide, with its familiar and comfortable Provençal design elements, deftly combines simplicity and luxury. It has the ease, low-key elegance, and muted palette beloved by French insiders who find the modest and unpretentious textiles and unadorned antiques to their refined taste.

During the summer in La Bastide, when the Shannons visit, Ducasse's traditional cuisine, with

vegetables and herbs from the inn's organic garden, is part of the draw. Travis and the young Shannons insist that Tracy's French-inflected seasonal cuisine comes close. For flavor and fragrance, the Shannons have ripe Meyer lemons, oranges, Hass avocados, and fresh herbs and lavender for the picking just outside the kitchen door—not to mention the markets of Santa Barbara for inspiration.

As the Shannons had seen on their visits, Peyrot infused the décor and the overall experience of La Bastide with Provençal authenticity and integrity. She commissioned designs on delicate dinner plates from a painter in Villeneuve, had the quilted bedspreads and curtains stitched up by a seamstress from Puimoisson, and celebrated the arts of Provence with custom-made baskets by an artisan from Forcalquier, casual glasses and tumblers by a talented glassmaker from Biot, and

bowls by a ceramicist from Salernes. And she found country antiques, all of them with a light touch, from antiquarians all over Provence, including special finds in Mouans-Sartoux and at legendary Isle-sur-le-Sorge. The Shannons followed in her footsteps.

It was the same search for authenticity that guided the Shannons when they searched for property around Santa Barbara six years ago.

"We had heard about a property for sale about ten minutes from downtown Santa Barbara," recalled Travis, a VP and financial adviser at Merrill Lynch. "It was seven acres of a flat plateau, with mounds of dirt. Other than five hundred healthy organic Hass avocado trees, it was very neglected. But the views out to the Channel Islands and the ocean were astonishing. And there was a feeling of peace and privacy. Tracy was willing to give it a try."

IN THE FLICKER OF AN EYE
(Opposite and Right)
Sunshine shimmering through the trees, the intense gaze of late afternoon light reflecting off the ocean, and fresh air with the scent of lavender—this could only be Santa Barbara (or Provence). The Shannons planned a comfortable window seat in the hallway leading to guest rooms, to make daydreaming an all-day affair. The pillows were crafted from vintage French textiles found in Avignon. A metal settee in the hallway was found at a Provence flea market.

Working closely with architect Christopher Dentzel and their general contractors, Giffin & Crane, the Shannons set out to capture the rustic elegance of the Provençal countryside. The goal was to work in the same traditional materials used for village and country houses in Provence: plaster, terra-cotta, stone, handmade glazed tiles, reclaimed French *parefeuille* tile, and limestone. The walls are thick, and the building has the heft of a seventeenth-century country house. The hands of local craftspeople are evident at every corner; tall ironwork gates, handsome stonework, and hand-applied plaster give a feeling of authenticity.

On one trip to France, the Shannons shipped back an oak farmhouse table, antique doors and mirrors, old armoires, Louis XVI–style chairs upholstered in natural linen, embroidered bed linens, country pine chairs,

painted shutters, and colorful pottery. Still, the effect is understated, true to the spirit of Provence, not tricked out and certainly not "theme" French décor.

"It is not really a stretch to re-create the south of France up here," said Travis. "The climate is very similar. In the summer, we have great bolts of lightening crashing across the sky, just like Provence. And we have the Santa Ana winds, the fierce mistral-like winds that bluster through here, just like the Luberon."

At La Bastide de Moustiers, the garden flourishes with olive and chestnut trees, cypress, rows of lavender, and rustic trellises filled with the blooms of pink and white centifolia roses.

In Santa Barbara, Travis and Tracy planted lemon trees in Anduze pots, two hundred cypress trees, eight hundred lavender plants, purple wisteria on a trellis, and

FIRES OF GALAXIES AND DREAMS (Opposite and Above) The brilliance of the Shannons' La Bastide inspiration was that the Provençal hideout they love is very family friendly. Rooms are casual and relaxed and confidently spare. The style was deftly transposed to the Santa Barbara interiors. In the living room a conversational group of linen-upholstered club chairs (monograms added in Santa Barbara), and a pair of fauteuils upholstered in natural linen, cluster around the fireplace of antique limestone, shipped from Provence. The fireplace surround is from Santa Barbara Stone. The lantern was acquired at an antiques shop in Cotignac that also sold the Shannons vintage quilts, pillows, and Provençal pottery.

GAUZED BY THE WINGS OF
BUTTERFLIES
(Opposite and Left)
The couple chose elaborate
heirloom linens from Aix-en-
Provence for their down duvet-
soothed bed. The carved bed was
shipped back from Moustiers-
Ste-Marie, along with the silver
sconces. Simple, handcrafted
terra-cotta tiles, in the authentic
Provençal spirit, keep their cool
on scorching summer afternoons.
An antique French country
caned chair offers the perfect
note of casual chic.

hardy rosemary. Stone tables on sheltered terraces make perfect vantage points for enjoying the fast-growing plants. And their private and very hidden acres are surrounded by 175 acres of Parma Park, a reserve with equestrian trails, an oak grove, sage, an olive grove, and wild chaparral.

For the family, the pièce de résistance in the garden is the swimming pool.

"I wanted it to be very simple, very tranquil and understated," said Travis. The family has a 360-degree view up and down the coast and across the surrounding hills and valleys.

In the early spring, the sunrise paints pale orange and pink splashes across the ocean and the western sky. Occasional visits by a young bobcat, prancing deer, eagles, and coyotes emphasize the natural setting that surrounds the property. King snakes occasionally slither through the rows of lavender, and in summer there have been reports of rattlesnakes.

Red-tailed hawks sail on thermals above the house, and two great horned owls perch and hoot on the chimney from April until late September.

"The owls are our alarm clocks," said Travis. "We set out to create a sense of Provence—but we ended up putting together a vivid and inspiring life that is the essence of California, with the happiest memories of France." ■

OUTDOOR LIFE (Opposite) Blessed with warm, sunny weather year-round, the Habers can swim most days. Michael added a series of sprinkler fountains around the perimeter of the pool to bring the sound of water to the garden, which overlooks rolling hillsides with few signs of other residences.

(Left) All of the doors and windows of the house were crafted by Southwest Doors & Windows of CA, in Santa Barbara, then painted and finished to have the appearance of an old hacienda. The company also made hand-forged hardware in the Spanish Colonial style for the doors and windows.

THE PLEASURES OF A HACIENDA

IN MONTECITO'S "Golden Triangle," the Haber family explores the many joys of childhood.

One weekend in summer 2004, Michael and Eileen Haber and their three young children headed north from Los Angeles for a welcome weekend break in Montecito.

Blissed out from the warm sunshine, family play in the surf, quiet roads, and the area's sense of gentility and calm, the Habers had an epiphany. Within days Michael, an in-demand photographer and filmmaker (clients include Microsoft, the Gap, Target, and *Departures* magazine) and Eileen, a model turned interior designer, had switched their life's focus to the Santa Barbara area, intent on making a new start among the equestrian

trails, parks, rolling hills, Spanish Colonial–style houses, beaches, gnarled old oaks, and fragrant gardens. They'd been feeling stressed out by the freeways and traffic of Los Angeles and decided they would be happy slowing down and downsizing.

"In a way, we decided to move on a whim, but then we got serious and made our working list of requirements for the house of our dreams," recalled Eileen. Included among their desires were that the house should be Spanish in style, all on one level, and with fireplaces and sheltered outdoor terraces. They wanted a rambling

ARCHITECTURE WITH A SPANISH FLAVOR (Right)
The front of the Habers' house, with its antique terra-cotta tile roof, was built in 2004, but with artful finishing and astute selection of materials it looks as if it has stood in Montecito for many generations. The adobe brick walls are painted white. The property is surrounded by mature oaks and evergreens, and the Habers later craned in hand-picked old olive trees. "The trees add life and a mystique to the house," said Eileen. "We feel very protected here."

indoor-outdoor house where the children could play in the garden and where they would have lots of freedom to come and go—and to spend time together.

"We were out looking one afternoon, and we came upon our ideal house—but it was all promise, a work in progress," recalled Eileen. Over a hedge they could see an adobe brick hacienda under construction, surrounded by pepper trees and handsome old oak trees.

"We peeked around the property, and quickly decided it was perfect," she said. "This house was sun-kissed. It seemed blessed in its location, with views in all directions."

The house was a spec renovation by Montecito designers Jon and Mary Lou Sorrell of Sorrell Design. Originally a 1940s ranch house, it was reshaped into an elegant hacienda, with Spanish-style doors and windows and a recycled terra-cotta tile roof.

The house is centrally located in Montecito, with views of the coast two miles away. Adjacent to a spiritual retreat and the San Ysidro Ranch resort, the land surrounding the house can never be developed.

"The Sorrells are geniuses," said Michael. "We started the process of acquiring the house. Finding and buying it before completion meant we were able to select reclaimed Spanish pavers for the floors, limestone pavers for the terrace. We were able to choose the paint colors and finishes that would be practical for a family. But we also wanted the luxury of white Carrara marble for the kitchen."

In the end, the house was almost custom built, with the talented Sorrells as trusted advisors and uncompromising professional guides. Details like the outdoor living room were finessed, with a large fireplace

where the family and friends can gather in the evening.

Exterior walls are real adobe bricks, a traditional Santa Barbara building material that gives a richly textured appearance but is infrequently used in the twenty-first century.

Eileen set to work furnishing the interiors with the Habers' favored bohemian cosmopolitan style. In this hacienda, there is no formality. From their travels—and from the rich hunting grounds of the flea markets, antiques shops, and design stores of Los Angeles, Santa Barbara, and Summerland—the family gathered antique Balinese beds, casual slipcovered sofas and chairs, vividly colored Chinese carpets, Fortuny silk lanterns, Art Deco bar accoutrements, Thai textiles, Italian bed linens, and vintage landscape paintings.

The children's art projects and paintings are displayed in the kitchen. Skateboards, basketballs, tennis racquets, rain gear, and dog toys have a way of piling up in the entry hallway.

The décor is a celebration of family. Michael's soulful sepia-print photographs celebrating spiritual subjects hang on the walls, along with the works of inspirational photographers such as Herb Ritts and the great French photographer Jacques-Henri Lartigue. Rows of family portraits taken by Michael are shown in antique silver frames, glittering and jewel-like on a mantel. Paintings by Michael's mother are hung in the dining room.

Almost all rooms of the U-shaped house open to the terrace, so there are always cross-currents of air. The family seldom turns on the air-conditioning. In winter,

the tile floors seem to retain heat, and the thick adobe walls are effective at keeping out the cold.

There is also a good dose of fantasy in the property.

In need of a private office, Eileen had the idea to build a canvas tipi beneath two oak trees in the garden. As it turned out, she found a corner of the house to turn into a practical workspace, but the tipi plan went forward. Nomadics Tipi Makers in Bend, Oregon, crafted a handsome and sturdy fifteen-foot-tall canvas tipi, complete with traditional Sioux painted symbols.

The family consulted with a Chumash tribe member living in Santa Barbara, who expertly installed the complex interwoven poles and lashed together the sturdy canvas tipi. Eileen furnished it with woven carpets, pillows, and mattresses for comfort.

"For me this house is a spiritual place, with magical crows in the trees, families of woodpeckers that live in the palm trees, mallard ducks that visit, hummingbirds feasting on the flowers," said Eileen.

On Sunday afternoons, the family piles into Michael's white 1958 Cadillac El Dorado convertible, luxuriating in the red leather interior, warm sunshine, and fresh air. The car, offering maximum enjoyment, seems to have been built for leisurely drives into the Santa Ynez Mountains and north to Ojai.

"We all work hard all week, so these Sunday drives out to the countryside are a great treat," said Michael.

And recently the Habers have added a guest house, a pool house, and a discreet garage extension, all with a Spanish Colonial aesthetic and completely consistent with the spirit of the residence.

"Living here, we are surrounded by peace and quiet and a feeling of harmony," said Eileen. "We definitely feel that we belong." ■

SPIRIT LEVEL
(Opposite and Right)
An eighteenth-century Mexican sculpture depicts Santiago (St. James) going to battle against the Moors. Haskell displays his collection of locks and keys from Spanish and Spanish Colonial chests, from the fourteenth to the eighteenth centuries, acquired for pennies during a Hearst Castle warehouse deaccession sale in the 1960s. Dance masks on the wall were handcrafted for Mexican and Guatemalan religious ceremonies. Around the top of the door is an eighteenth-century carved and painted Peruvian door frame.

A CELEBRATION OF SPANISH COLONIAL TRADITION

IN SANTA BARBARA, Michael Haskell lives with rare Mexican and Peruvian antiques and paintings, and colorful Talavera pottery.

The family of antiques dealer Michael Haskell goes back more than four generations in Santa Barbara. Haskell, owner with his son, Eric, of Michael Haskell Antiques in Montecito, said that his family instilled in him a strong sense of the history of the region and when he was in high school he started to study and collect Spanish Colonial antiques and American Indian textiles, rugs, and beadwork.

A favorite aunt who lived in Guadalajara encouraged his interest in Mexican antiques, and on holidays there he began his lifetime collection of expressive Talavera pottery, ex-voto paintings, and early colonial furniture. He founded Michael Haskell Antiques in 1968, specializing in Native American basketry and rugs, and Spanish artifacts and furniture from colonial times.

In 1980, he and his wife, Kim, acquired five acres of land at the end of a long, winding road in Pedregosa Canyon. The site, in the Santa Barbara foothills, is above the summer fog line, so it is always sunny.

The floor plan and first phase of construction for the two-story Mexican hacienda was initiated with the assistance of architect Larry Clark.

"Larry and I grew up surfing together, so we sat down with a glass or two of wine and worked out the

RECOLLECTIONS OF A LIFETIME
(Left) Rose the black Labrador
poses in the living room of Michael
Haskell's hacienda. The plaster walls
were painted by Kim Haskell with a
rich wash of terra-cotta paint, and
ceiling beams were hand-adzed to
give the room a sense of age and
heritage. An eighteenth-century
Spanish Colonial table from Peru
offers shelter to a pair of nineteenth-
century China trade chests made of
painted leather over camphor wood
frames. Haskell's lifelong collections
of seventeenth- to early-nineteenth-
century Talavera pottery from
Puebla, Mexico, are displayed around
a China trade chest.

orientation and basics on a piece of paper," said
Haskell. "Our concept was to craft a house in the
traditional Mexican family ranch style, surrounding
a central courtyard."

To give the house a sense of authenticity and
integrity, the Haskells brought back richly detailed
architectural fragments from Peru, Guatemala, and
Mexico. They also incorporated handcrafted doors,
reclaimed terra-cotta floor tiles, old windows, hand-
forged hardware, painted wood cabinets, and
forged-iron sconces and chandeliers, all with a
rustic style. Rust, chipped paint, and the patina of
age were part of the attraction.

The family's antiques collections include Talavera
pottery, vivid and haunting religious paintings from
small-town basilicas, as well as sombreros, musical
instruments, kitchen tools, farm implements, tiles,
books, and textiles.

"The house is a very comfortable retreat, twenty
years later," said Haskell, an ardent surfer who still
joins his high school and grammar school friends
at Haskell's Beach on mornings when the surf is
up. "But it's the Mexican antiques that give it its
true soul." ◼

THE GRACE OF HISTORY (Opposite and Above) In a guest room, an early-twentieth-century Mexican painting hangs above a headboard made from an altar railing of a demolished Peruvian church. A colorful hand-embroidered Mexican shawl makes a vibrant bedcover. A wall of eighteenth-century Mexican ex-voto paintings on tin and on linen canvas, created to give thanks for miracles and intercessions performed by saints, were acquired in small towns near Guadalajara and Mexico City.

DREAMING OF THE OLD WORLD

EQUESTRIENNE/INTERIOR DESIGNER YOLANDA HADID created an elegant family home in a former horse trainer's quarters of a Montecito estate.

It was probably inevitable that interior designer Yolanda Hadid would create a European-style house on her gated property, surrounded by a two-acre garden in the heart of Montecito.

Hadid was born in Papendrecht, a small town near Rotterdam in Holland. She was discovered by a scout from the Ford Modeling Agency at the age of fifteen and began a highly successful career in Paris, London, and New York almost immediately. After working on a photo shoot in southern California twenty-five years ago she

dreamed of living near Santa Barbara.

"I traveled the world for fourteen years as a model, heading to far-off places like Tokyo and Tahiti for dreamy fashion shoots," recalled Hadid, still model-svelte and photogenic after years away from the camera. "It was a wonderfully nomadic life, and I've seen every luxurious and beautiful place. I arrived in Santa Barbara, saw the beautiful setting, and immediately I knew that one day I would live here."

Today she lives two minutes' walk from the center of

DISTANT HEMISPHERES (Opposite and Above) An antique horse carriage Hadid found in France has come to rest in the cobblestone courtyard of the house. It's filled year-round with lavender, geraniums, and petunias in terra-cotta pots. The stucco exterior of the house is adorned with iron lanterns, and Hadid enlarged an upstairs bedroom with French doors that open onto a small forged-iron balcony.

Montecito with her three children, with occasional visits from the girls' horses, Captain Hook, a brown Welsh pony, and Prince Phillip, a gray Welsh pony.

"Horses were part of my childhood, and my children are horse-crazy. Being surrounded by some of the finest equestrian facilities and trainers in the world is one of the great attractions of this region," said Hadid. "Growing up, I rode Dutch Warmbloods, which are bred to be great jumpers, superb for dressage, very athletic, and with a wonderful temperament. They are considered the

Bentleys of the horse world. I spend a lot of time taking care of our horses at the stables, just a few moments from our house. We get dusty and dirty from the riding ring, and we come home happy and tired. I designed the house for precisely this kind of relaxed, sporty life."

Hadid first found her Montecito property in 2000. "It was on a former ranch property, very American, very simple, very functional. It had probably been built as a simple barn for a groom, a farm manager, and finally a horse trainer," she said.

She imagined a villa, a Spanish Revival house, with warmth and traditional European character.

Working with her former husband Mohamed Hadid's Los Angeles–based construction company, Hadid Development, was key to achieving her dream. Her building crews moved into the house, adding hardwood floors, plaster walls, marble floors, and custom woodwork.

"I had a fantastic crew of specialist plasterers, wood carvers, stone masons, all with old-world talent," she said.

While they were working on every inch of the house, she was in Europe finding antique architectural details, such as carved wood doors, and the authentic furniture that add integrity and character to an interior.

"The goal for me is to have a loving and warm family home," she said. "Here we have a very outdoor life, and we are often in riding clothes. We approach horse riding, exercise, and competition as a discipline, and always wear the correct outfits for the sport. Our boots are clean, at least when we begin, and we wear gloves. We have great respect for the elegance and traditions of equestrian sports."

The move to Montecito made their outdoor, horse-riding life possible.

"Life in Montecito is warm and very friendly," said Hadid. "We go to the grocery and we see our friends. Families live here. We are five minutes from school and from the horse barn. That's important. Raising horses is an every-day job."

Hadid also has a thriving business, through her Hadid Interiors company, building and developing properties and furnishing them with rare European antiques. ■

CHAPTER FOUR
THE BEACH LIFE

The broad swaths of beaches of Santa Barbara invite exploration
from early morning to sundown. Living along the ocean's edge is
the ultimate California dream. Surfing is a lifetime passion.

CASTLES IN THE AIR
(Opposite and Right)
Nina Terzian aimed for a pale palette for her beach house. In the living room, the board-and-batten walls, a cane wingback chair, and her antique French scallop-shell coffee table were all given the white treatment. The dramatic fireplace was improvised with a pair of carved wood mythological dolphins, topped with a series of carved moldings stacked to form a bold mantel, all painted white. The fireplace surround is a large slab of lapis lazuli, a recommendation from Christina Da Ros of Santa Barbara Stone. Decorator Peggy Gouger, a longtime friend, also helped Terzian brainstorm on décor. Oars and other flotsam and jetsam were irresistible to Terzian. "Whenever I see anything nautical or marine, such as antique ship lanterns or shells, I have to have them for my house."

AND SEA AND CLOUDS BEYOND

WITH CONFIDENT ENERGY and a light-hearted sense of style, Nina Terzian turned her Miramar Beach house into her own homage to coastal living.

Former Chicago resident Nina Terzian never intended to live full-time at the beach in Santa Barbara.

Like many dedicated Santa Barbara residents, she arrived from the Midwest for a wedding.

"I came, I saw, I moved here," said the high-spirited Terzian.

Around a decade ago, she acquired a beach cottage on the sand on Miramar Beach, adjacent to the Miramar Hotel.

"I was going to live in it while I renovated another house," she said. "But then I slowly started painting and fixing up the beach house. The more time I spent there, the more I loved it.

Miramar Beach is one of the treasures of Santa Barbara, and easily one of California's prettiest beaches: its golden sand somehow always clean, the beach is sheltered and inviting at all times of the year. There are just twenty-six residences lining the beach, and no possibility for new construction.

Terzian's cottage is so close to the historic Miramar Hotel that when it reopens after a period of restoration she promises she will be able to order fresh oysters or a salad from room service, and they will arrive in minutes, chilled and ready to enjoy.

"I bought the house for the great location," she said. "It was a '70s building, very boxy and rather cold. But I'm right on the sand. I saw the possibilities of making the house feel warmer, more like a cottage."

She enlisted architect Anthony Spann and contractor Mitch Williams to reshape the interiors, and to add character with new decorative details, board-and-batten walls, and all-new woodwork.

When the construction was completed, Nina Terzian headed to Summerland, a beachside town nestled between the cities of Carpinteria and Santa Barbara and noted for its wealth of antiques galleries.

"I found most of my furniture and antiques at the Summerland Collective," she said.

Terzian had owned luxury retail stores, including Montblanc and Louis Vuitton in Chicago, and is currently co-creator of the wildly popular Only Hearts Club doll collection, distributed internationally.

Wood floors were installed, hand-planed, and hand-finished to resist sand. All woodwork was painted white, and most of the furniture is white. Sofas and chairs have easy-going slipcovers in ticking stripes.

From the living room, Terzian can gaze across the water to the blue silhouettes of the Channel Islands and a cluster of oil rigs silhouetted against the sun-struck water.

"At night, with the rigs' operational lights twinkling across the sea, it looks like Christmas lights, surprisingly festive," said Terzian. (Oil drilling along the coast is now very restricted. A 1969 oil spill catastrophe was the catalyst for the emergence of an active environmental movement in the Santa Barbara area, which many cite as the birth of the modern environmental movement.)

For Terzian, the beauty here enriches her life, and lifts the spirits of fortunate family and friends who visit.

"I wanted the house to feel as if I am in the south of France or in the Greek islands, on permanent vacation," she said.

"My routine here at Miramar Beach is to have no routine," said Terzian, who is often joined at the beach by her daughter and three young grandchildren. "I have not taken a vacation since I acquired the house more than ten years ago. I can't imagine anywhere that is better than this. My one regret is that I did not come here sooner. This is paradise." ■

REFLECTIONS ON THE WATER (Opposite and Above) Nina Terzian was attracted to the large-scale, white-painted three-part antique mirror and had it moved to her house from the Summerland antique shop where she found it. The movers set the mirror up temporarily on the floor of her bedroom, and it has stood there ever since. She saw that it would make the perfect headboard, reflecting the ocean waves, the beach, and the Channel Islands in the distance. "The mirrors bring every mood and change of light from the sea into my bedroom," said Terzian. Her third-floor bathroom, also whitewashed, enjoys private views of seagulls, surfers, and a glamorous swath of the beach.

PARADISE FOUND

FORMER ANGELENOS Jules Allen and Richard Goldstein discovered the delights of a modernist house perched above legendary Butterfly Beach.

Their love affair with a house began by chance, said Richard Goldstein and Jules Allen.

Taking a favorite weekend break at the Biltmore Hotel in Santa Barbara with their three daughters, the couple was strolling along Butterfly Beach, a handsome swath of sand and sea that's a favorite of locals.

"We saw a tiny 'For Rent' sign, almost hidden in a hedge," recalled Richard, whose firm, Company, produces television commercials for Nike and Coca-Cola.

The spacious house for rent, a classic 1950s modernist masterpiece, was one they had admired for years. On the spur of the moment, the couple (Jules Allen runs Allen Allen, a sportswear company, and Jules Allen, which offers cashmere tops in forty vibrant colors) rented the property.

"We became the total beach family, heading down to Butterfly Beach every morning," said Allen. "The girls

CHANNELING THE 1960S (Left) Vivid collections of midcentury glass spike the light-filled living room, with its space-age fireplace front and center. Allen and Goldstein formerly lived in a modernist house in Palm Springs, and they took full advantage of the desert city's design stores and vintage arcades like the Galleria to find a George Nelson bench, a Saarinen Tulip table, Blenko glass, Murano hand-blown glass, and a favorite treasure, their dramatic blue glass floor lamp, designer unknown.

learned to ride bikes on bike paths near the house. In Los Angeles we lived ten minutes from Santa Monica Beach, and we never went there. It took moving to Santa Barbara for us to realize how much fun beach living can be."

They also got to know nearby ultraprivate Montecito, which reveals itself slowly and discreetly.

"Since we've moved to this area, we've discovered historic estates, private properties behind tall iron gates and long driveways, wonderful accomplished friends, and superb local restaurants," said Allen. "And we happily make the ninety-minute drive to Los Angeles offices so that we can live here." Paradise indeed. ■

FUN HOUSE (Opposite and Right) David and Sue Peterson made a fortunate purchase with their board-and-batten beach cottage. Two decades ago, it had seemed like the perfect first house, to live out the honeymoon, fix up, and then sell. As they added to the house (without changing its modest vibe), they also groomed the garden and installed dolphin-adorned window shutters. They brought the living room its neutral palette and an easygoing style that welcomes sandy feet and wet swimsuits, and legions of sun-bleached-blond athletes of all ages.

AMERICAN IDYLL

FOR THE ATHLETIC PETERSON family, proximity to Miramar Beach, tennis courts, and swimming pools—and relaxed days at home—spell a perfect life in Santa Barbara.

Twenty years ago, when they were first married, champion athletes David and Sue Peterson acquired a charming turn-of-the-century cottage within easy reach of downtown Santa Barbara and near Montecito. Built originally as staff quarters for a nearby mansion, it was surrounded by palm trees and just seconds from the beach.

The Petersons, who were married at Fernald Point in Montecito, had thought they would remodel it, sell it, and move up to a larger house. But after a few years of happy domesticity, and three children, the family could not imagine letting it go. They added French doors opening onto the deck and installed new, larger windows to embrace the sunshine. And over the years they have redone the kitchen, added a master bedroom suite, remodeled the home office, and built lofts and guest rooms for their frequent visitors.

The house, almost like a clubhouse on weekends, is sheltered by tall hedges, and David has installed over the years a basketball hoop and backboard, a climbing wall, a trampoline, the family's popular home theater in a former garage, and a tree fort—to complement a growing

SUMMER SCENE (Opposite and Above) Like the chill-out setting for a scene in a classic '70s surfer film, the Petersons' house is decorated with shells collected from beaches around the world, garden flowers in vintage jam jars, and Lakey's surfer girls' cheering section. Even the outdoor painted claw-foot bath on its enclosed private deck seems like a throwback to an earlier hippie-dippie era when innocent pleasures were part of the California dream.

selection of trail bikes, tennis racquets, and surfboards for the whole family.

It's the classic California lifestyle story. Dad David, a champion of youth sports, is an ardent marathoner; Sue, a champion swimmer, is still a keen surfer, and she heads out early most mornings when the surf is good. From an early age, the three children (who were home-schooled at several points) were involved with athletics at school, and in the water.

While pregnant with her younger daughter, Lakey, Sue used to swim a mile off Butterfly Beach each day. Now teenaged Lakey is a fast-rising champion surfer, both aggressive and graceful, who also dives into water polo and has played on a boys' football team. Son Parker is a water polo star. And elder daughter Whitney, studying at the University of Southern California, is a national tennis champion.

The Petersons' house has offered a light-hearted setting for all these athletic activities. It's small but has been the base for a life of travel, accomplishment, and enjoyment, with grandparents, friends, team members, and fellow surfers all gathering on the terrace for Saturday dinner, or post-point-break gatherings to watch movies. ■

CHAPTER FIVE
CALIFORNIA COUNTRY

Few places so elegantly celebrate and express the love of
horses and their architecture than the Santa Barbara area.
Noble Lusitanians and Andalusians and the purest and most
refined of thoroughbreds are adored, honored with elegant
stables, and pampered, as they deserve.

LINES OF RESONANCE
(Opposite) Illuminata, a young
Andalusian, waits patiently beside
the stable colonnade. The English
antique copper vat will be turned
into a trough and fountain for the
horses. Incandela and Schoelkopf
planted olive trees in the graveled
courtyard to offer shade for the
horses, and to ground the
architecture. The colonnaded side
of the building is buried beneath
the ground to make it less
imposing in the landscape.

EQUINE EXERCISE
(Right) Gerald Incandela walks
Illuminata (affectionately called
"Lumi") around the property as
morning coastal fog lifts and the
day becomes warm and sunny.

SPANISH TRANSLATION

ON A HILLSIDE NEAR SUMMERLAND, artist Gerald Incandela and garden enthusiast George Schoelkopf built the most elegant stable/studio, honoring the noble Andalusian horses that inspire Incandela's world-acclaimed art.

When artist and photographer Gerald Incandela first arrived in Santa Barbara from New York in 1994, he was not overcome by the expected appreciation and adoration for the architecture of the region. These came later.

"I didn't originally appreciate or understand the Spanish-inspired architecture and the traditional Spanish Revival residential styles in Santa Barbara," he said. "They seemed watered down from the rigor and energy of the original Spanish style. Soon, as I studied the superb achievements of George Washington Smith and other legends of Spanish Revival architecture, it all started to make sense. It absolutely grew on me. There is nothing less than handsome in Santa Barbara. It simply never misses."

Incandela, a true world sojourner, has family roots in Sicily. He grew up in Tunisia, then a French protectorate, and later studied in Paris before exploring Berlin, Rome, and London and eventually finding himself studying art in New York City.

"I tried every European capital, it seems, before settling in the United States," he admitted.

Incandela and his partner, former Manhattan

antiques dealer George Schoelkopf, who has degrees in art history from Yale University and Columbia University, eventually acquired an eleven-acre property on a hill above the coast near Summerland.

The property was very neglected, but the location and its mild climate suit George, a garden enthusiast who had previously nurtured and designed Hollister House garden in Connecticut, recently acquired by the Garden Conservancy.

"There was nothing here, not even a tree," said Schoelkopf. "It was just dried grass, very sad-looking. It was the views and the microclimate that made it spectacular."

The partners built a Spanish-style residence and a few years ago, after Incandela became interested in Andalusian horses, decided to build a stable with a space for his studio and darkroom.

The stable was designed to define the top of a wind-swept hill, and to create a sense of boundary and shelter to the property, called Montalba.

To research the architecture, Incandela and Schoelkopf pored through rare architectural folios of historic Andalusian and Venezuelan country houses and barns, as well as Spanish colonial stables.

"For us it is more than a stable," noted Schoelkopf. "For us it's sculpture, an architectural statement with beautiful horses inside it. Well, for Gerald, the horses are the important elements."

It was George Washington Smith who inspired the arched colonnade, as well as the substantial proportions of the columns, which are crafted from cast concrete shaped and finished with stucco.

Incandela's photography and drawings, homage to his equine muses, are in the permanent collections of many prestigious museums and galleries, including the Metropolitan Museum and the Museum of Modern Art in New York. They are shown at Edward Cella Art + Architecture in Santa Barbara.

And the barn/stable is a constant uplift and inspiration.

"We see the massive form of the stable across the courtyard, so it is a constant presence in our lives," said Incandela. "It frames the landscape beautifully." ∎

BENEATH A VAULTED SKY

LIFE IS ENJOYED in the outdoors at remote Folded Hills Ranch, where Kim and Andy Busch and their energetic children enjoy sporty weekends on horseback.

The way Santa Barbara residents Kim and Andy Busch recall it, for two years they had been looking for a "romantic" country property with charm, old gnarled oaks, privacy, a creek running through a valley, and not forgetting a house with character.

"We had expressed all of our hopes and dreams to the realtor—and told her we also wanted open spaces for exercising and riding Andy's horses, lots of room for our children," recalled Kim. "We looked at a lot of great properties, but had not seen anything that was right. Finally, our realtor took us to a remote corner of the Santa Ynez Valley. We drove onto the property in early spring and fell in love with it the moment we headed up the driveway."

Golden afternoon light flickered through an allée of pepper trees. They glanced over oak-covered hills rolling down to a flat valley. As they headed toward the main house, they saw a lake framed with cattails. They later found it was a favored habitat for snowy egrets, hawks, California quail, and several endangered species of birds.

At the end of the driveway of Folded Hills Ranch, they saw the white plantation-style house that had originally been built in the twenties by Joy Morton, the Chicago-based founder of Morton Salt, who sequestered there in the winter.

Ironically, the Busches were not able to view the interior of the house that day. The doors were locked. They peered into the windows, and saw a handsome stone fireplace, hardwood floors, and were pleased to see that the interiors were in their original state, and had not been modernized.

They immediately acquired the farm and the

family now drives up there every Friday afternoon from Santa Barbara.

"We discovered that the house and property were very neglected and run down, and the house especially needed a fast infusion of care and attention," noted Kim. Over months, they carefully repaired and polished—while carefully retaining the relaxed and casual air that had first attracted them.

The residence sits in a prime position surrounded by mossy old oaks, with rolling hills as backdrop. The family often rides out into the property above the house to watch the sunset flash through the trees. Out there, with beef cattle grazing in the distance, no houses or roads are visible.

"We think the Morton family must have stayed there only in the summer because the house was not very well insulated," noted Kim. "We've fixed that. In the Santa Ynez Valley in winter it's cold. Our horses have frost on their backs in the early morning."

Fog rolls in from the ocean, the air is chilly, and ethereal drifts of breath rise from the pampered horses, which prefer to roam free outdoors.

Barns, outbuildings, a horse ring and hills for roaming are important to Andy Busch. He the son of August Busch Jr., former chairman and chief executive of

Anheuser-Busch, and is the great-grandson of brewery cofounder Adolphus Busch.

A national polo champion, he has been the highest-ranking American amateur in US professional polo.

Kim Busch particularly loves the farm in April when the hills are "Leprechaun green," she avers. Soon, as days become warmer, the golden days of summer turn the hillsides golden, shimmering in the heat.

The ranch, hidden and private, has made just one semipublic appearance, in 2005—as the setting for the ultraprivate surprise wedding of the actress Sandra Bullock and her beau, *Monster Garage* television show host Jesse James.

Arriving at the farm in a red monster truck, Bullock and James were married in a sunset ceremony at the Folded Hills Ranch. As Sandra walked down the aisle a taped recording of her late mother singing Bellini's aria, "Casta Diva" floated in the valley air.

"Sandra chose the ranch because it is so private, so protected, almost impossible to find," said Kim. "It's not a pretentious farm, and it suited her perfectly."

The Busches, who travel the world, and enjoy polo games in Palm Beach, Palm Springs, Boca Raton, and Argentina, like their low-key days at their farm.

On weekends, Andy and his sons repair fences, go

fishing in the well-stocked lake, or work out on the polo field, exercising the polo ponies and preparing for the season. Andy, who had been riding since he was very young, took up polo when he was sixteen.

It was only natural that the family would move to Santa Barbara, which has one of oldest polo clubs in the United States. The Santa Barbara Polo & Racquet Club is also one of the finest polo clubs in the world.

Andy is on polo fields six months of the year, often working out with members of his team, Grant's Farm Manor. The three young Busch sons often play in the kids' polo tournaments.

After the intensity of workouts or a game, the peace and tranquility of the ranch becomes especially appreciated.

Out in the 350 acres of Folded Hills Ranch, Andy has encountered endangered white ospreys (no doubt attracted by fish in the lake), golden eagles, mountain lions, bobcats, and herons.

Andy's thoroughbreds, former stars of the race track, roam the hills and pastureland surrounding the house

and have shown a marked disdain for barns and shelter the Busch family offers. Resident managers, grooms, and expert farmhands keep close control.

In their farm sanctuary, the family also keeps a menagerie of rare and domestic animals, including miniature Sicilian donkeys, llamas, rabbits, pet turkeys and guinea hens, goats, miniature horses, an emu, and Andy's favorites, Greater Swiss Mountain dogs, a tribute to his Swiss-born mother.

In the fall, the weather is hot during the day and the family spends hours outdoors, working, hiking, riding, and swimming.

"We enjoy all of our holidays at the ranch," said Kim. "At Christmas we decorate the whole house, and it's very traditional, very family-oriented. We love it."

Kim is also serious about the family's responsibilities in protecting their land.

"We are stewards of this great property, and, in a humble way, it is our life's work," she noted. "Our children will continue to improve and take care of the land and animals, keep it all in the California ranch spirit." ∎

PHOTO CREDITS

ACKNOWLEDGMENTS

This is my fourth book with Rizzoli. Each book was initiated when the brilliant and insightful publisher, Charles Miers, issued a resounding "Yes." I especially appreciate Charles's encouragement of a unique concept, an eccentric and individual focus, and a definitive approach to each new book. With a glance and few perfectly chosen words, Charles sets the tone, polishes the vision, and defines the concept. Essential.

Special, heartfelt thanks to senior editor Dung Ngo, who worked closely with me in Los Angeles and New York as I selected film, planned layouts, and constructed this book as a lively and colorful—and unexpected—portrait of the Santa Barbara region. Dung has a profound and worldly understanding of design and architecture and style, and he is a witty and wise collaborator. Assistant managing editor Lynn Scrabis stepped in with great professionalism to give the book a perfect and graceful ending. I appreciate her quiet approach to book production—and her hard work. Liana Krissoff edited the text with an unerring eye and light touch.

When I first proposed the concept of a book on Santa Barbara, working with the superb photography produced for *Santa Barbara* magazine, Jennifer Smith Hale, the dynamic president and editorial director of *Santa Barbara*, and the founder of *C* magazine, was immediately enthusiastic as she had always wanted to publish a book showcasing Santa Barbara. Jennifer has championed my concept and followed through with elegance, quick decisions, vital charm, and encouragement.

Jenny Murray Hooks, a fantastic ally, collated material from years of *Santa Barbara* issues and created a compelling collection to preview and select. Warmest thanks, Jenny.

I owe extreme gratitude to the photographers—Lisa Romerein, Luca Trovato, Tim Street-Porter, Danica Perez, Langdon Clay, and Michael Haber—whose superb images are presented here. Lisa Romerein, in particular, has an unerring and highly original vision, and her photographs give readers an up-close and fresh introduction to every detail in a room. I have always admired the way her work captures and crafts mood and nuance. Bravo and thank you, Lisa.

Once more I am so pleased to be working with the great art director Paul McKevitt and his team at Subtitle. Paul's elegance, polish, sense of perfection, and professionalism contribute enormously to the finished book. I am deeply grateful.

The exceptionally talented editors of *Santa Barbara*, for the last decade, have captured, shaped, directed, and perfected a broad range of design, architecture, and garden features that drew my attention. This devoted group of people are the experts on the Santa Barbara region, and it was their work and insights that made this book possible. The originality, quality, and freshness of their approach glisten on each page of this book. Heartfelt thanks to all, especially Gina Tolleson and Gina Zondorak Terlinden.

To all the homeowners, and the designers, architects, artists, craftspeople, philanthropists, surfers, equestriennes, antiques dealers, landscape designers, and Santa Barbara–area talent whose work and creativity and deep love and appreciation of Santa Barbara are apparent on each page—bouquets and thanks. I am truly grateful.

DIANE DORRANS SAEKS

INDEX